Heroes and Charlatans
of the Savannah

Nick Ngazoire Nteireho's **Heroes and Charlatans of the Savannah**, is an in-depth analysis of how many west and central African countries strived, struggled and mostly, for internal and external reasons, failed to provide their citizenry with more prosperity than turmoil.

Nteireho grounds his words with vignettes about his home, Uganda, whose history reflects how African nations evolved under brutal colonialists, visionaries that possessed more paranoia than uplifting ideas, and in recent years heartless efficient authoritarians.

The author knows African politics and writes about it with tough objectivity that at its essence, despite all, remains hopeful.

Frank McCoy is a Maryland-based journalist who has written about West, South and East Africa, and now covers Science/Tech for STEMRules.com.

A tour de force, this book provides snapshots of key watershed periods, actors, and actions in Africa's checkered political history from the time of major external incursions in the Continent. Written with accessible and riveting prose, the book brings to light the promises and perils, hopes and tragedies of a complex Continent that defies easy conclusions.

Moses Khisa, Assistant Professor of Political Science and Africana Studies, North Carolina State University.

Heroes and Charlatans of the Savannah

Nick Ngazoire Nteireho

LitPrime
"Your story is our priority"

LitPrime Solutions
21250 Hawthorne Blvd
Suite 500, Torrance, CA 90503
www.litprime.com
Phone: 1-800-981-9893

Published by LitPrime Solutions   11/29/2022

ISBN: 979-8-88703-095-1(sc)
ISBN: 979-8-88703-096-8(e)

Library of Congress Control Number: 2022920018

CONTENTS

CHAPTER 1

The great migration of wildebeests, zebras, and gazelles from the northern Serengeti in Tanzania to the Masai Mara in Kenya, is a familiar sight to nature lovers. As thousands of animals run and stampede to cross the Mara River, their journey is fraught with incalculable danger. Giant crocodiles, perhaps, alerted by the rhythm of trotting hooves, lie in wait, to grab and drown the first unfortunate one that meanders into their path.

For those that manage to cross the river, their ordeal is far from over. Packs of hungry lions, cheetahs, hyenas, and wild dogs, all take turns to isolate many of the migrating animals, and pounce on them, once they have lost the safety of the crowd. Meanwhile, scavenging birds soar in the skies above, waiting for the opportunity to descend and strip the last morsel off the bones of carcasses left behind in the scorching tropical sun.

This is the full cycle of nature, and its attending pecking order. But on the Serengeti plains, order is never strictly observed on a seniority basis. That fierce-looking maned lion, whose portentous presence makes most other animals jittery, may be forced to surrender its zebra carcass to a pack of mean-spirited hyenas or wild dogs, if only to avoid a deadly bite from their razor-sharp teeth. Worse still, that hungry lion better not stare menacingly at the baby buffalo calf in the presence of its mother, for to dare come close may earn the king of the jungle the comeuppance of a broken rib from the mother's horn. And there are no animal hospitals on the plains of the Serengeti. Even the elusive leopard, perhaps the most adept hunter of all the big cats, doesn't always get his way. An old, dejected baboon, striving to impress a former lover carrying his brood, may climb a tree in which a leopard is perched, to harass and chase it away in order to mollify the lover's anxiety from danger, earning back the lover's confidence, and allowing the jilted one to be reunited with his family.

Yet life must go on. When the dry season scorches the grass and most plant leaves wither in the Serengeti Park during the hot months between November and January, the animals follow the rain pattern to the north, that provides them with greener pastures. Each morning, as one gazelle suckles its newborn calf before cautiously wandering off in the grassland, she's unaware of who was watching, and there's no guarantee that she will be around to feed her young in the afternoon. Up there in the open sky, the monstrous scavenger birds surveying the plains in satellite-precision fashion, can swoop down and snatch the baby gazelle, just another meal to feed its chicks in its nest atop the canopy of the baobab trees. Oftentimes, both mother and child will have been eaten by some predator before the day is over. Mothers in western Uganda have a lullaby called "Oyonke nkushereke", meaning, suckle quickly so I can hide you (from predators).

The survivors must produce calves during this migration, which swells the numbers that will eventually reverse the migration back to the original starting point. This theater of operations has played itself over thousands of years. Nature has always been and will continue to be unforgiving. It's a survival of the fittest.

To quote the character of boxer Rocky Balboa, played by Sylvester Stallone in the Movie Rocky,

In the 2006 sequel, Balboa tells his son: "The world ain't all sunshine and rainbows. It's a very mean and nasty place, and … it will beat you to your knees and keep you there permanently if you let it. … But it ain't about how hard you hit. It's about how hard you get hit and keep moving forward…"

That's how life has always been on the African Savannah.

The Olduvai Gorge is a valley stretching about twenty-five miles, formed when an earthquake drained an ancient lake, thereby exposing nearly two million years of history. It's located in northern Tanzania, within the Great East African Rift Valley, about 200 miles southwest of Nairobi, Kenya. Although Olduvai has been part of this theater since the dawn of history, its importance wasn't recognized until the 1950's, when an English couple, named Louis and Mary Leakey, made it the center of their archaeological research.

Louis Seymour Leakey was born to English Missionary parents in a small village west of the Kenyan capital of Nairobi on August 7, 1903. As a young man, Louis was taught at home by English tutors, while he spent his pastime hunting and trapping animals with Kikuyu youths, whose language he spoke like a native. He even went through Kikuyu initiations and rituals, including the one that required him to build his own house at age thirteen. World War One delayed his travel to England to study, but after the war, he entered Cambridge University, where he studied archaeology.

Mary Nicol who was ten years his junior, and later became Louis' second wife after his divorce in 1936, was more privileged, with a father who took the family to the south of France, where he painted pictures that he sold in London. Her rebellious nature made her quit elite Catholic schools in London by age seventeen, eventually settling for courses in archaeology.

Louis' interest in archaeology started forming in his early teens, after he came across ancient relics such as axes curved out of obsidian materials, which differed from flint ones found in Europe. The first fossils of Neanderthals were discovered in Germany in 1857, followed by Cro-Magnon in France in 1868. Then Java Man was later discovered in Sumatra, Indonesia in 1894, enhancing the belief that, homo sapiens must have evolved either in Europe, or possibly in Asia about

60 thousand years earlier. Until his pioneering work in the Olduvai Gorge demonstrated that fossils of homo sapiens found here were older than those found elsewhere on earth, racist attitudes that prevailed in the scientific community, and print media such as Joseph Conrad's "The Heart of Darkness", denied the possibility of tracing the origins of man to the so-called Dark continent of Africa.

The East African Rift Valley is a giant fork-like geological **plate, whose eastern prong runs up from the mouth of the Zambezi River in Moza**mbique, through Tanzania, Kenya, Ethiopia, to the Red Sea. The western arm runs from Malawi, through western Tanzania, Burundi, Rwanda, and Uganda, trapping the Great Lakes of the region between these countries and the Democratic Republic of Congo.

The Leakeys' important discoveries in the Olduvai Gorge, attracted many other archaeologists to take interest in the East African Rift Valley. After Louis Leakey died of a heart attack in 1972, his wife Mary soldiered on, with assistance from Richard Leakey, one of her three sons. However, the most spectacular discovery was made in 1974, at Afar, in the Ethiopian section of the Rift Valley by Donald Johanson of Case Western Reserve University. The partial remains of a female skeleton he and his team found were dated to be 3,2 million years old. These were the oldest hominine bones ever discovered anywhere. Johanson named the fossil Lucy, after a Beatle song they listened to in their camp the night of the discovery.

In 1976, Mary sealed the Leakeys' legacy with the discovery of man's oldest footprints at Laetoli, 35 miles from Olduvai. The set of hominine footprints was preserved in volcanic soil, dated to be between 3.59-3.77 million years old.

Toasted and honored at many universities around the world, Mary died in Nairobi, Kenya, in 1996 at the age of 84. Her granddaughter Louise, Richard's daughter, continues to carry the baton in search of human origins.

Tanzania has also long provided the backdrop to the studies on primates by world renowned primatologist and anthropologist Jane Goodall since setting up camp in Gombe National Park in 1960. The park is located about ten miles north of the regional capital of Kigoma, and is close to the sprawling Lake Tanganyika, which, at 4,823 ft, is the second deepest lake in the world after Lake Baikal in Siberia, Russia (5,387 ft).

CHAPTER 2

The institutions and practice of slavery and serfdom have been going on across all civilizations for millennia. Many societies kept slaves for one reason or another, sometimes acquired through inter-tribal wars, but in other cases, enslaving people from within their own societies. No region of the world was spared from this scourge. The Egyptian pharaoh's power was viewed through the grandiose edifices such as the pyramids, which he built using free slave labor. In pre-European Americas, the Aztecs and Mayans kept slaves, as did the Sumerians and Babylonians in the near east. Roman armies are known to have raided and captured slaves in territories we now know as Britain, France and Germany.

Serfdom, a condition akin to slavery, where an individual, or an entire family can be held in perpetual servitude to a feudal lord, still permeates societies in Asian countries up to now, especially in the Indian sub-continent. In 19th century Imperial Russia, close to one third of the peasants, called krepostnoy krestyanin were serfs treated as chattels like the American slaves. They were freed by Emperor Alexander II in 1861, three years before Abraham Lincoln emancipated the slaves in the US.

On the African continent, Arab traders had been plying the East African coast for 1000 years before Europeans appeared on the scene. They traded in cloves from Zanzibar, but also hauled ivory and slaves from the mainland. Regarding the latter, however, unlike the European slave trade in West Africa which shipped their human cargo to the Americas, to toil in sugar, cotton and tobacco plantations, those captured on the east coast and the central African hinterland ended up being used as sailors and pearl divers in the Persian Gulf, soldiers in the Oman army, and laborers in the salt mines of Mesopotamia (present day Iraq). Others were shipped off to the Indian sub-continent, to be used as laborers in unsavory chores such as leather tanning, considered beneath the status of higher castes. The black Dalits of India, descendants of African slaves, are part of the wider so-called untouchables, the lowest caste in the Indian pecking order.

It's no secret that African kings and chiefs had been conducting slavery over some of their subjects, and people captured during inter-tribal wars. In West Africa, Ashanti and Benin chiefs raided neighboring villages for slaves long before the Europeans started commercializing it. The chiefs used some of the slaves in their armies, while others were deployed as farm laborers and domestic servants. The increased demand for cheap labor in the Americas escalated slave trade in West Africa, to the extent that, some of the captives included former slave raiders themselves.

In his research on African slavery, Abdulaziz Yusuf Lodhi of Uppsala University, Sweden, quotes King Gezo of Dahomey as having said,

"I'll do anything the British want me to do, so long as it does not involve stopping me from dealing in the lucrative slave trade". That was between the period 1818-1858, during which the British had launched a serious anti-slavery campaign.

Commercial slavery in East Africa predates that in West Africa by many centuries. Arab traders had established trading posts along the coast, and even built settlements on the islands of Zanzibar and Pemba, long before Vasco da Gama sailed along the coast on his first voyage to India in 1493. Intermarriages with African coastal peoples created a new group known as the Swahili, who became the ruling class, and still dominate in the political economy of the area. Trade became so lucrative for these Sultans and Arab merchants, to a point where, rulers like Seyyid Said, once the Sultan of Oman, moved his capital from Muscat to Zanzibar. Once they settled, they opened interior trading posts in such far-flung areas as Tabora, Ujiiji and Kigoma on Lake Tanganyika, and Mwanza on Lake Victoria, all located in present day Tanzania. Later, the Portuguese also brought in slaves from Southeast Asia, mostly from India, Malaysia and Indonesia. The majority of these were women, brought in as domestic servants and concubines.

High demand for commodities such as ivory, rhino horn and minerals by India, Europe, and the Americas, drove traders further inland, escalating further demand for labor to haul the merchandise to the coast. Slavery continued unabated even after it was abolished and declared illegal by the British in the early 19th century. Portuguese slave ships, in attempts to avoid detection by British Naval patrol ships in West Africa, started fetching their human cargo destined for Brazil, from their colonies of Angola and Mozambique. The French also continued the trade to supply cheap labor for their newly established sugar and coffee plantations in Mauritius, Reunion, and Madagascar.

While the slave merchants were usually people of different nationalities such as Arabs, Persians, Indians and Europeans, the suppliers were almost exclusively, local chiefs, and any local groups who benefitted from the trade. In East Africa, these included Prazeros from Mozambique, descendants of Portuguese fathers with African mothers, who operated along the Zambezi River. Other prominent groups included the Yao of southern Tanzania and northern Mozambique, operating northeast of the Zambezi River. The Yeke under Chief Msiri of Katanga collaborated with Chief Mirambo of the Nyamwezi to establish a short-lived raiding station at Urambo around Lake Tanganyika, in 1860, extending their raids into southern Angola. In Kenya, tribes such as the Kamba aided in the slave-raiding effort, while farther north, the Amhara and Oromo collaborated in capturing Somali groups, according to historian Yusuf Lodhi.

Serious attempts to abolish slavery in England and elsewhere, started in 1771. By the 1780's, religious groups such as the Quakers, led by

Granville Sharp, launched campaigns to abolish slave trade. At the same time, abolitionists such as William Wilberforce lobbied the British Parliament regarding the resettlement of the freed slaves back to Africa.

However, these were soon overtaken and overwhelmed by other events, such as the American declaration of Independence in 1776, that either directly aided this effort, or completely changed and shaped its direction. Also, beginning in 1789, and stretching for the next ten years, the French Revolution under Napoleon Bonaparte, introduced radical social changes based on the troika concepts of **liberté, égalité, and fraternité** which were not in conformity with slavery. This in turn, helped curtail the power of monarchies and churches, and inspired democracy, not only in Europe, but in other parts of the World, especially, the nascent American republic.

For France, the coup de grace about its slave activities in the Caribbean came in the form of a slave revolt of 1791 at Saint Domingue in present day Haiti, which drove out slave owners, and resulted in the declaration of independence in 1803.

Last, but not least, the advent of the Industrial Revolution in Britain, and demands for free trade, coupled with the expansion of trade into Asia, required implementation of new efficiencies that slave labor could not provide. In the West Indies, the British government declared the buying, selling and transportation of slaves, illegal in 1807, although it allowed ownership to continue until 1834. At that time, children below six years were all freed, while adult slaves were declared apprentices who could work for six years without pay, only receiving food rations. But apprentices were treated as badly as slaves, and finally, this system too, was abolished in 1838.

Many former slaves had no alternative places to go, and chose to stay on the same plantations, working for low wages. Plantation owners were compensated to the tune of 20 million pounds for the loss of their slaves, a colossal sum at that time. These owners would, however, soon replace the slaves who left with indentured Indian laborers.

Attempts by British abolitionists to end slavery in the United States of America were met with a lot of resistance from southern slave owners. Instead, they turned their sights on ending slavery in India and East

Africa. Their efforts were complimented by luminary figures like Dr. David Livingstone, who suggested using the three Cs of Colonization, Christianity, and Commerce, going so far as advocating for territorial occupation by the British Crown to fully take control.

In East Africa, following the Anti-Slavery Treaty of 1822, the abolitionists put a lot of pressure to bear on slave traders in the region. Although the process dragged on for a long time, eventually, traders like Sultan Seyyid Barghash of Zanzibar, finally agreed to sign a treaty on June 5, 1873, which made slave trade illegal in areas he controlled. The Heligoland Treaty, signed between Britain and Germany in 1890, declared Zanzibar a British Protectorate. The same year saw the signing of the Brussels Conference Act, also known as the Slave Trade Treaty by Western European countries. This treaty targeted the suppression of slave trade, and the importation of alcohol and firearms into Zanzibar. Both of those items were used as currency between traders and chiefs, in exchange for slaves in the East African hinterlands.

With pressure mounting on slave trade, owners sought to exploit the intricate relationships that existed between master and servant. First, the anti-slavery treaties were not seriously enforced by the British, arguing that based on the West Indies experience, sudden disruption would cause severe lawlessness and damage to Zanzibar's well-developed plantation economy. Second, although following the 1890 Treaty, which allowed Zanzibar slaves to buy their freedom, few of them could afford to do so.

Plantation slaves had one to three days a week to either till their own plots, or work for someone else for wages. Neither of these activities was lucrative enough to earn the amount of money needed to purchase their freedom. Even after the government agreed to pay owners compensation for the loss of their slaves, most didn't leave the plantations. Some of the reasons that kept the slaves on the plantations included, ignorance about the laws, intimidation by former owners, and fear of losing rights to cultivate their plots.

It is worth mentioning that occasionally, slave owners freed some slaves on their own free will, depending on the social status the slave occupied in the owner's household. The ex-slave (mhuru) might then be declared a son, or brother by the owner (bwana/mwinyi), and if a concubine, then declared a wife, and the children legitimized. Most slave owners granted these freedoms as last acts to thank Allah (God) as they aged, or prior to going or upon return from a Hajj to Mecca. Sensing the end of slavery, shrewd owners encouraged former slaves to buy their own freedom by donating pieces of land owned by slaves through the kiambo system of communal land ownership. This in a way, ensured that the slave and his family would remain attached to his former master.

There was a little bit of sugar-coating when researchers like the late Professor Ali Mazrui, in his PBS Series, "The Africans", painted the picture, that despite the brutality associated with slavery, especially for those working on plantations, and runaways, in the Swahili society, and Arab countries, domestic slavery was relatively benign. They go on to say, that an ex-slave could virtually rise to any status. For instance, it is known that of the six governors of Zanzibar appointed by Sultan Seyyid Said before moving his headquarters from Muscat to Zanzibar, two of them were ex-slaves of Ethiopian descent. But when it's all said and done, truth be told, that even in those Arab societies where ex-slaves were integrated into the family, the dark ones have never been fully embraced enough to occupy that empty seat at the table.

However, institutionalized slavery remained until 1904 in Kenya, 1909 in Zanzibar, and 1919 in Tanganyika, after Britain acquired the latter, following the defeat of Germany in the First World War. The traditional version of slavery held out in countries like Nigeria, until 1936, and even later until 1942 in Ethiopia. Modern day slavery continues to thrive in countries like Mauritania, Mali, Sudan, Chad, et cetera, not to mention the Indian sub-continent, where serfdom has been practiced for centuries.

CHAPTER 3

I t's been more than fifty years since the majority of African countries gained independence from their colonizers. Yet, despite having gotten rid of the colonial yoke, no other region of the world still laments about the negative vestiges of colonialism like the African continent.

Colonization in Africa reached its peak between the mid-1800's and early 1900's. During the Berlin Conference of 1884-85, European powers sought to draw clear demarcation lines over territory each would control, to prevent future conflicts. Among the European powers, Britain, and France, together, controlled about two thirds of the continent before WW I, increasing their share to more than seventy percent after WW II.

After World War I, Germany, the vanquished aggressor in the war, was stripped of all its territories, which were parceled out and shared by the victors under the League of Nations arrangement. Tanganyika, (the mainland part of Tanzania) was taken over by Britain, Rwanda and Burundi, the other part of German East Africa, was allocated to Belgium, while Namibia (South-west Africa), was to be administered by South Africa.

Many reasons are floated about why Europeans were stepping over each other in their quest to have a piece of the African continent, Starting with Prince Henry the Navigator of Portugal (1394-1460) who sent out sailors in search of gold, spices and other treasures, Europeans were captivated by what lay beyond the blue, including some wild stories about the Dark continent.

The late Professor Ali Mazrui, a renowned scholar about the impact of colonialism on Africa, advanced three main reasons for European fascination with Africa. First, Africa as an unknown entity, paused a special challenge for the scientific community, about which they wanted to gather new data. The first explorers such as Morton Stanley, Samuel Baker, Richard Burton, and David Livingstone etc., were mainly geographers, news reporters and scientists. The reports they submitted back home upon return, usually contained claims of having discovered many natural wonders such as mountains, rivers and lakes. Problem with these wild claims was that it was the natives who had taken the strangers to gaze at sights that had been known to generations of the natives' forebearers.

Dr David Livingstone was one of the pre-eminent figures of the British colonial and exploration era. Born March 19, 1813, in Blantyre, Scotland, he trained as a physician at Charing Cross Hospital Medical School from 1838-40. His father Neil, a traveling tea salesman had wanted to limit David's studies to theology, but he failed to suppress his son's intellectual curiosity between science and religion. Readings like Karl Gutzlaff's Appeal to the Churches of Britain and America, helped David convince his father about the symbiotic relationship between science and religion. After immersing himself in theology, Latin and Greek, he applied, and was accepted by the London Missionary Society, under whose banner he became an explorer and missionary during the reign of Queen Victoria.

Livingstone was persuaded by Robert Moffat, an LMS missionary, on leave from an outpost in South Africa, that he was the right man to take on such a job in Africa. He accepted, and took on the role of a crusader, advocating for the anti-slavery movement, by pushing for abolition through a combination of missionary work and expansion of the British Empire using commerce. He set out on an African voyage to resolve what had puzzled the geographers of the period, establishing the source of the mighty River Nile. He believed there was a link between Lake Tanganyika, one of the great lakes in the western prong of the rift valley, and the Nile River. This, however, would later be proved wrong by other explorers. By solving this mystery, he also believed, this would render his name enough prestige to end the Arab slave trade in East Africa.

He first settled at Mobutsa mission in present day Botswana which he abandoned in 1845, following disagreements with a fellow missionary named Roger Edwards. In 1847, he abandoned another station at Chonuane because he was in the crosshairs of the Boers who were amid their voortrekker north. His next settlement was at Kolobeng, where he converted Chief Sochele in 1849, who only lasted a few months before lapsing back to his traditional beliefs. Journeys he took further north convinced him that effective evangelization would only happen if Africa was opened to European commercial plunderers and missionaries.

Between 1852 and 1856, he traversed and explored territories further north, covering the entire length of the Zambezi River, becoming the first white man to witness "Mosi-o-Tunya", or smoke that thunders, which he subsequently named Victoria Falls in honor of Queen Victoria. He remarked that the falls were "so lovely, the angels must see them during their flights". He was also the first white man to make a trans-continental journey from Luanda in Angola to Quelimane on the mouth of the Zambezi. Unlike other European explorers of the day, Livingstone negotiated, rather than forcing his way through territory. He also traveled light, with a few servants who carried some artifacts he bartered for food. This factor, coupled with the fact that he used persuasion rather than force for his evangelism, allayed fears among the chiefs he met, that he was on a conquering expedition. His mantra became one of the three C's (Christianity, Commerce and Civilization), which he believed would dislodge and wipe out the Arab and Portuguese slave trade.

Livingstone returned to Britain to campaign and garner more

support for further exploration of the African interior. He even resigned from the London Missionary Society, who wanted to restrict him to missionary work. The British government agreed to fund a second expedition to explore the navigability of the Zambezi, which he had failed to establish during his earlier travels. It later turned out that the river had cataracts and rapids at Cahora Bassa that made it unnavigable. Today, this site hosts a giant hydroelectric dam that supplies power to both Mozambique and South Africa. During this expedition, Livingstone was also assessed to be a poor leader, incapable of leading a large-scale expedition. He was described as moody, secretive, and intolerant of criticism, all qualities that constrained such an undertaking. He went back to Britain in 1864, but returned to Africa in January 1866, this time to search for the source of the Nile.

Unlike explorers such as Richard Burton, John Hannington Speke, and Samuel Baker, who had guessed its location to be somewhere between Lake Albert and Lake Victoria, Livingstone believed the source laid further south, on Lake Tanganyika. Henry Morton Stanley and John William Shaw had been sent by the British government to persuade Dr. Livingstone to return home. But when they arrived at his station post at Kwihara, Tabora in northwestern Tanganyika, he had left for Kigoma, near Lake Tanganyika in his quest to find the source of the Nile. Stanley and Shaw decided to follow Livingstone to Kigoma. However, twenty miles out on their way, Shaw contracted malaria and diarrhea forcing him to return to Tabora. His condition got so bad, and lacking the basic ingredients for treatment, in desperation, he shot himself to death. Stanley proceeded on his journey during which he met the famous explorer at Ujiji in 1871, eliciting the memorable quotation, "Dr. Livingstone, I presume".

The two men returned together to Kwihara, where they paid tribute to their fallen compatriot. Stanley stayed for a few months with Livingstone in Tabora, during which he failed to convince him to return home. On March 14, 1872, Stanley left Tabora for Zanzibar, where he would catch a steamer to sail back to England. In August of the same year, Livingstone decided to head south in search of Lake Bangweulu in northern Rhodesia (Zambia). He rode a donkey, while accompanied by his two servants, Chuma (Tanzanian) and Susi (Sudanese) who walked on foot. He had liberated them from slavery and paid each about 5 East African shillings per month. On the way, Livingstone was taken ill with Malaria, and making matters worse, his donkey died of exhaustion. He was carried to Chief Chitambo's village at Ilala, near the Lake Bangweulu swamps, where he died on May 1, 1873. Per his instructions, his heart was removed and buried under a mpundu tree. The rest of his remains were salted, preserved, and then carried by his faithful servants to the missionary station in Bagamoyo, from where the body was shipped back to England and buried with honors.

The second reason put forward about colonialism is rooted in the need for missionaries of major religions such as Christianity and Islam, to acquire and spread their faith to new converts. African societies which were governed by their own traditions and beliefs, were initially very resistant to the intruder, trying to impose foreign, and incomprehensible beliefs upon them. However, given the prevailing European ethnocentric view of superiority over the African, this conversion usually took a brutal approach, giving true meaning to the song, "Onward Christian soldiers matching as to war". This initial approach is well-dramatized by the forceful christening of "Kunta Kinte" to Toby, in the classic movie "Roots", based on Alex Hailey's book of the same name. Missionaries such as Dr. David Livingstone adapted a softer approach, winning over converts by administering medicine which healed the body first, before attempting to heal the soul. Variations of this approach were later implemented in different countries, building clinics for the sick, and schools to train locals in administrative procedures and European languages which helped the colonialists further their causes.

The third reason advanced is based on "European Imperial Grandeur", with each power attempting to outdo its rival by acquiring and showing off its new possessions. Adventurers like Karl Peters curved out Tanganyika for Kaiser Wilhelm II, Cecil Rhodes acquired a large chunk of territory in the south (Rhodesia) constituting current Zimbabwe and Zambia for the British Crown, while King Leopold of Belgium, one of the most esurient characters in colonial history, got himself the biggest prize of all with the acquisition of present-day Democratic Republic of Congo, then named Congo Free State, with an area more than forty times the size of his tiny kingdom.

As Mzee Jomo Kenyatta, the first president of Independent Kenya once put it,

"When the Europeans first arrived, all they had was a gun and a bible while the African had the land. They gave him the bible, told him to close his eyes and pray. By the time he opened his eyes after the prayer, his land was gone, and all that was left for him was that bible, which he could hardly understand".

The three reasons mentioned above are interrelated in many ways. Any scientific knowledge gathered about a specific region would allow an imperial power to assess whether or not to allocate further resources for a particular purpose. A resource rich region may, for instance, call for immediate plans to create roads and railways to exploit the natural resources. Instinctively, if their interests were threatened, as in situations where exploitable resources were found, but faced unfriendly local resistance, troops were immediately deployed to quell riots and protect advance teams, be they missionaries or colonial administrators. This aspect of colonization ultimately always called for close collaboration between sponsoring agents such as the Royal Geographical Society, or voracious, greed-driven entrepreneurs like Cecil Rhodes, and the imperial state. Rhodes, an ardent supporter of colonization, had a grand vision of constructing a railway line, running from Cape Town to Cairo, through British territory. Like the explosives merchant Alfred Nobel who turned his evil trade into the nimble Nobel Peace prize. Cecil Rhodes turned his into the coveted Rhodes scholarship, administered by none other than Britain's premier University of Oxford.

A symbiotic relationship existed between the bureaucracies of the colonialists and the missionaries who followed them. While the missionaries set up the schools and hospitals, including control of the curriculum, these were financially subsidized by the colonial administrations. And, in case of a riot, colonial soldiers were always at the ready to step in quickly to suppress the uprising. The entire aim of the colonialists was to bring both body and soul of the African into total submission. The school curriculum, for instance, taught subjects only from a Euro-centric perspective, suppressing all aspects of African culture, including punishing students for using native languages. In my own elementary/primary school, teachers used "a counter system", akin to issuing a yellow flag in football/soccer to caution and punish errant students who used vernacular language instead of English.

In the Catholic church, for instance, mass was said in Latin by predominantly white priests. The congregation of mostly illiterate and half-baked natives only participated in singing and rehearsing meaningless hymns. Christianity emphasized submissiveness and forgiveness "for transgressions of those who trespass against us". African customs were scoffed at, and looked down upon as primitive, their religious beliefs declared evil and devilish. Christianity also put more emphasis on the afterlife than the present, which it considered temporary. Humiliation and other indignities inflicted upon the colonized subjects were deemed to be cleansing and ennobling. All these actions were purposefully calculated to alter the African mindset into believing in his less self-worthiness vis-à-vis his European/white counterpart.

There's no doubt that the education provided by colonialism liberated millions of African minds and provided many with the skills that enabled them to ascend to higher standards of living they could never have acquired otherwise. But this was achieved to the detriment of the African culture and values, vital ingredients which future independence freedom fighters would find missing. The creation of "a black Frenchman" through the French policy of assimilation epitomized the ultimate in indoctrination, where the black man was taught to believe that by abandoning his African culture, he too could be fully French. They even went as far as saying that "the French don't care who goes to bed with who, so long as they both speak French".

But the hollowness of this concept was in full display during the

International Football World Cup in Moscow early in 2018. When the French team won the coveted prize, the French people whose politics had recently been mired over Marlene Le Pen's hatred for immigrants, didn't know whether to address as French, the heroes of the team such as Kylian Mbappe, the 19-year top scorer, together with the more than half of the team, composed of recent migrant players from former African colonies who constituted the French team. Yet, when an illegal 22-year-old immigrant from Mali, named Mamoudou Gassama, scaled a high-rise building on a Paris Street in spider-man fashion to rescue a French toddler from falling to his death in May 2018, he was aptly feted at the Elysee Palace, and instantly awarded French citizenship by President Emmanuel Macron.

Oftentimes, the education of the natives swung the pendulum in favor of the colonialists, creating the cultural acclimatization desired. The Kenyan Independence period Attorney-General, Charles Njonjo (dubbed Sir Charles) exemplified this. A British-trained barrister, his impeccable pin-striped Saville Row suits, with a top hat, and a British wife to boot, made him appear to have more in common with the real Prince Charles in London than his Kikuyu and Luo compatriots.

One joke making the rounds at that time on his Anglophile infatuation excesses, quoted him as having had this exchange with a fellow cabinet minister upon visiting the friend's wife in an upscale Nairobi hospital,

"Who is your wife's doctor?", inquired Sir Charles.

"Dr. Mwangi", replied to his friend.

"How can you put your wife's precious life in the hands of an African doctor?", quipped Sir Charles, with a disturbed look on his face, whereupon his friend shot back,

"Isn't it sad that the entire nation entrusted its laws with this African?", referring to Sir Charles. The African doctor Sir Charles had just disparaged was a top-notch specialist in his field, and one of a few in the country at that time.

Colonialism was partly driven by imperialistic motivations of large countries wishing to dominate and influence less powerful ones. Capitalistic aggrandizement of accumulation of wealth was pushing European powers to flex their muscles beyond their borders in competition with each other. As it has always been throughout the ages, he who has more tends to command the respect of his peers. On the economic front, it was soon realized, that, with the dawn of industrialization setting in, European industries could not sustain the pace of their production with only the raw materials sourced from their countries. Nor could they sell the surplus production in their countries. Therefore, whoever could access a steady supply of inputs and markets, would, ultimately, sooner or later, dominate in the marketplace, and by extension, become the dominant power. Imperial powers could tap into their newly acquired reservoir of cheap human resources abroad, not only to produce inputs for the burgeoning factories, but also to fight wars such as WWI & II, that would have been untenable with their populations alone. Britain, for instance, recruited a lot of soldiers from its African colonies to successfully fight against German aggression during the second World War.

Beyond the imperial aspect was the cultural obligation of what Rudyard Kiplinger called "the white man's burden", This process would involve enlightening and civilizing the so-called primitive races and making them see the light, pushing them towards the realms of a life only the white man had created and continued to champion since the dawn of civilization. Some saw this as a calling, a passion manifested by a destiny, akin to God creating man in his own image.

Senator Henry Cabot Lodge, in a speech justifying the US expansion of its territorial control to both the Caribbean and the Philippines, put the white man's burden concept in more colorful, albeit racist tones. He alluded that "the US didn't become a great power by accident, but rather, was driven by the spirit of our race, whose mighty movement westward conquered and built a nation from the Atlantic Ocean to the Pacific Ocean". Taking over the Philippines, he implied, would take this movement closer to the edge of the cradle of the white man's Aryan ancestors, where it all began. More recently, another white Congressman, Steve King from Iowa, echoed these sentiments. In a speech, he questioned why people should consider the term white supremacy as vulgar, going as far as suggesting that "no other ethnic group has contributed to modern civilization as we know it, apart from white people".

Modern philanthropy and the related concept of Noblesse Oblige, where the wealthy and privileged feel compelled to help the less fortunate have borrowed and improved on Rudyard Kiplinger's original white man's burden concept. However, there is a difference in approach between how colonialism delivered its services, compared to the way philanthropists like the Bill and Melinda Gates deliver theirs.

In Africa, life under a colonial setup constituted a bastion of highly segregated services in almost all aspects of life. School systems, where they existed, were segregated by race, especially at the lowest levels, allowing for a little semblance of integration towards the top rungs such as technical institutions and universities. It was common in cities like Nairobi, Harare, Johannesburg, or Kampala, to find European, Asian and African schools run separately by the same Ministry of Education. There wasn't even a disguised attempt to call it separate but equal, as was the case in the US before the 1954 landmark case of Brown versus the Board of Education. Perhaps, more than anything else, housing in cities by far displayed the sharpest disparities for the different racial groups.

The best exclusive places were usually reserved for Europeans/whites, while Asians, the next group on the social scale, occupied whatever accommodation existed downtown, mostly apartment units above their business premises. The black natives were relegated to the poorest forms of housing, located in swampy, malaria-infested areas of the city, or simply left to crowd out in tin-and-wood shacks on the outer edges of the city. Thus, we have estates like Muthaiga and Karen in Nairobi existing in parallel with ghettos like Kibera and Mathare valley, or the upper-class neighborhoods of Groenkloof and Waterkloof of Pretoria, versus the township of Mamelodi. In some colonies such as Kenya, Zimbabwe (Southern Rhodesia) and South Africa, entire regions of the country were declared white settlement areas, and off limits to African natives. Occasionally, an uppity black might be allowed to settle in the white area under very strict conditions.

Most hotels employed Africans as servers and laborers, although hardly any blacks stayed there, not only due to a deliberate discriminatory policy from the white managers, but even more so from being priced out. This attitude persists up to today, with upscale hotels in Nairobi, such as Stanley Hotel or Norfolk Hotel staff (Africans), frowning at potential black guests, reminding them how expensive the hotel is. The situation is even more magnified in South Africa, considering its more recent racial attitudes. Public transportation, especially trains, were demarcated into first, second, and third classes, allowing price discrimination to eliminate most natives from the first two upper classes. The famed "Blue train" that traverses between Pretoria and Cape Town with high-rollers doesn't offer services to low-paying passengers. Whether educated, professional or not, the black man's social status was not to be equated to that of an English gentleman.

Unlike the French colonial system, where well assimilated Africans such as the late Senegalese President Léopold Sédar Senghor, and his Ivorian counterpart, Felix Houphouet-Boigny served in the French Parliament, the British made no such provision. Even while preparing their colonies for independence, they could not conceive of a situation where the Africans could practice debate in the British Parliament, for, to do so would convey a sense of equality, something that never crossed their mind. To the British, the concept of Britishness was only acquired through ancestry and culture.

In countries with significant British/white settler populations, such as Kenya, Zimbabwe and South Africa, the colonialists ensured that there were two sets of laws, one for the whites, ensuring dominance in almost all aspects of life, and the other set for the natives. Under the French colonial system, while they equally despised the African as uncivilized, they nevertheless allowed a system of egalitarianism to flourish within French suzerainty. The system allowed a kind of "supervised autonomy" for the colony, where the French had to dominate such issues as the economy, foreign affairs and the military. Francophone countries in West Africa, for instance, were united under the CFA franc, tied to the French franc, with no single country determining its own monetary policy. At the same time, the French maintained a sizeable contingent of military gendarmerie in each colony, to ensure that Paris would always call the shots at the first sign of trouble. After 1946, the French system allowed Africans to participate in French political affairs at three levels, namely, country, regional, and metropolitan. Once fully acculturated, a man or woman could be considered French irrespective of ancestry.

The contrast between the French and British colonial systems is clearly illustrated by the way they treated two prominent African citizens of the colonial era in the twentieth century.

Leopold Cedar Senghor (1906-2001) was born in Senegal and attended catholic missionary schools there as a young man. He later proceeded to France, graduating in philosophy and literature at the Sorbonne. With his acclimatization, he soon involved himself in the French political system, rising to serve as a minister in several governments of the day in the 1940's. His marriage to a white woman may have caused an occasional stare here and there but was not directly opposed by the French government. It was as if the French expected any self-respecting man like him to marry a French woman, who, in all probabilities, would have been white. He later served his home country of Senegal with distinction, even putting his philosophical training to work by penning the concept of 'Negritude", based on his life's duality as both a Frenchman and an African, partly to highlight the racism he faced as a black man living in a white man's world.

Seretse Khama (1921-1980) was destined to be king of the Bamwangato, the dominant ethnic group within the Batswana. But his father, King Sekgoma II, died when young Seretse was less than five, leaving the people to appoint his uncle Tshekedi Khama as regent. Like Senghor, he started schooling in (British) missionary schools, later attending the predominantly black college of Fort Hare, and then moving on to the University of Witwatersrand, both in the highly segregated South Africa. Returning to Bechuanaland (present day Botswana), briefly, he soon traveled to Britain, where he enrolled at Oxford University to study law and economics.

Ruth Williams was introduced to a young Prince Seretse Khama by her sister during a dance at Nutford House organized by the London

Missionary Society. He was, at the time, studying law at Inner Temple after Balliol College Oxford. They shared a common interest in jazz, and soon fell in love. The year was June 1947. Their plans to marry would, however, soon run into headwinds from both the British government and his own people, led by his uncle Tshekedi, who was his regent. His uncle claimed that the Bamwangato needed to have a say regarding the wife taken by their future leader. The British, on the other hand, feigning the racism behind the act, hid their objection by covertly supporting the protests forwarded by the governments of the two white-led governments of South Africa and Southern Rhodesia (Zimbabwe). The couple married at a registrar's office in London in September 1948, after the Bishop of London said he would approve of a church wedding only if the government approved. South Africa had just introduced the apartheid system that same year.

A meeting convened by the Bamwangato leaders in Bechuanaland, which approved Seretse as their King, and Ruth as their future Queen, did not sway the British government to do likewise. Determined to keep him off the throne, they lured them back to London in 1950, where they kept them in exile until 1956. They were only allowed to return after Seretse renounced his right to the throne. Upon returning as private citizens, Seretse founded the Bechuanaland Democratic Party, which won the elections in 1965 that catapulted him into the presidency. He was installed as the first president of Independent Botswana in 1966, thereafter, winning successive re-elections until his death in 1980. It is also quite telling that the same British government which denied him his birth right as king, knighted him soon after winning the presidency. Blessed with three boys and a girl, the second born, Ian Khama, born in 1953, the only one born during the parents' exile in London, also became president of Botswana, serving two terms, beginning in 2008.

The love story between Ruth Williams and Seretse Khama has now been immortalized into a hit movie. "A United Kingdom", starring Oscar award-winning British-Nigerian actor David Oyelowo as Seretse Khama, and Rosamund Pike as Ruth Williams.

About the so-called French enlightenment, Frantz Fanon, a black man who grew up on the island of Martinique, believing that he was French, and later moved to Paris to study Psychiatry, was shocked by the mistreatment and ferocity exacted on those who resisted France during the Algerian war for independence. The French, who openly wondered, "How can anybody be proud of being black?", also didn't take kindly to prominent writers of color such as James Baldwin and Langston Hughes, who had flocked to Paris, escaping racism in countries such as the US, but now opposed the French crackdown in Algeria. To Fanon, it became clear that a person of color could only become French by committing cultural suicide, whereby one fully embraced French culture by entirely disposing of his old culture. Rather than being guided by enlightenment and tolerance, it appeared that the treatment of their subjects in the colonies was mainly motivated by self-love.

While segregation was de rigueur for all the colonial experience in Africa and elsewhere, the rules applied by individual powers varied greatly. Both the British and French attempted to create a "European African" in their own image, although they never intended him or her to be a social equal. Nevertheless, the institutional framework they set up became widespread in territories they controlled, allowing for large scale acculturation and skill acquisition by different layers of Africans.

The Portuguese and Belgian colonial approaches in Africa differed significantly from those of either the British or French. In Angola and Mozambique, the Portuguese introduced a form of civilizing mission known as "lusotropicalism" which injected culture and ancestry by having Portuguese men sire children with African women, creating a new class of mixed race known as mestizos. This process was mostly a one-way approach that did not allow African men to have children with Portuguese women. However, without the force of the law to back this cultural mingling, most biracial children were abandoned by their fathers, and could not necessarily identify with Portuguese culture as intended. It would also appear that the fact that Portugal was less industrialized and affluent than its northern neighbors, rendered its colonialists more sympathetic to poor societies in the tropics. Nevertheless, the Portuguese still viewed themselves as being superior and above Africans. They even instituted a state policy forcing natives to work in sugar and coffee estates under very strenuous conditions.

The Portuguese colonialists created a pyramid structure of full-blooded Portuguese at the top, mestizos with limited privileges in the middle, leaving the bulk of the natives segregated and exploited at the bottom of the rung. Under the Portuguese system, an African qualified as civilized only if he/she spoke Portuguese, was gainfully employed, and had discarded all tribal customs. The Assimilados within the native population fared better than the Indigenas. The latter were expected to carry passes at all times, akin to the black experience under apartheid South Africa. Their indignities touched all aspects of life, including observing a curfew in towns, exclusion from sending their kids to public schools, and segregation in most facilities such as restaurants, hospitals etc. As more colonial settlers took residence, even the assimilados lost their privileges, paving the way to wholesale segregation. It's no secret that, compared to their anglophone and francophone counterparts, by the time they obtained independence from Portugal, the six lusophone African countries were less prepared to govern themselves.

Of all the 19th century European colonialist, tiny Belgium had outmaneuvered everybody, and walked away with the Congo, a territory ninety times its own size. On the face of it, King Leopold II's motives were aligned with those of fellow colonizers at the time. Among other reasons, he wanted to inculcate the benefits of civilization by developing the country, expanding on personal liberty, discouraging polygamy, and introducing native education. As in the case of Portuguese colonies with assimilados, the Belgians introduced a vague concept of evolues, referring to those who had been transformed from savagery and witchcraft to the Belgian idea of civilization. To qualify for this status, an African would have to be educated (in missionary schools), exhibit good behavior, and disassociate himself/herself from such evils as witchcraft. But the standards set were so vague, and the delineation so malleable that between 1948 and 1953, only about 500 Congolese were deemed qualified.

For Belgian settlers who detested the idea of even socializing with the evolues, they introduced yet another level called immatriculation, to tighten the rules. To be accepted in this civilized status, an African would have to be totally immersed in European culture, including fluency in the French language. His relatives and friends were interviewed to check his conformity to the norms ascribed, and his residence thoroughly inspected, including the bedroom and bathroom. However, all this decorum seemed to be cover up for the primary reason underlying their presence, which was wealth and profits. King Leopold II used the cheap supplies of rubber from the vast Congo forests to gain advantage in the expanding bicycle, and later automobile markets. But the Congo, then and now, was endowed with unimaginable natural resources, including precious minerals, the exploitation of which made the king tremendously wealthy.

The Catholic church was in cahoots with the colonial administration and mining companies in the exploitation of Congo's natural resources with no accountability. Companies hired militias which invaded villages to recruit workers for rubber and mining companies. Resistance to these militias often resulted in chopping off the culprits' hands, which they took back with them to show the bosses as proof of their serious recruiting efforts.

Belgian rule in the Congo was so roughshod, that it found its way into the daily lexicon of neighboring countries. In Uganda, for instance, to tell someone, "ori omubirigi", conveyed a sense that the person was very cruel. Of all the European colonial powers, only Belgium didn't seem to have a specific purpose about its post-colonial era. It would appear, that theirs was meant to be colonialism with no end in sight. So, when the Congolese agitated for independence, the Belgians who had no exit strategy, left in a hurry, unleashing the chaotic environment that has haunted the country until now.

The British governed their territories under a system of Indirect rule. First devised and practiced in Nigeria by Captain Frederick Lugard in the 1890s, it relied on co-opting existing local leaders such as chiefs and hereditary rulers through a combination of coercion and bribery, to be part of the colonial administration. Where a vacuum existed, the colonial administrators filled it by appointing their own "puppet leaders". The chiefs in turn received perks, including a salary, a house, protection, and gifts for keeping the people in line on behalf of the white colonial administrator. My recollection of this as a young kid in western Uganda, is that of sometimes my elder brother and I, accompanying my father to our county headquarters town of Rukungiri, to listen to the white district commissioner (DC), clad in white, and addressing the crowd through an interpreter (called entafuta).

At the apex of the colonial administration was a governor, appointed by the colonial office in London. He (almost exclusively men), reported to the colonial secretary. Among other exploits, the British used indirect rule to preserve ethnic identities, stemming away from national consciousness and awakening. At the same time, they encouraged ethnic rivalries which they alone could settle. To keep the ethnicities off balance, the colonial administrators would impose a person from a different tribe or region on another group even when this individual didn't understand their language or customs. Social welfare within the group was allowed, but political organizing was discouraged. Captain Lugard became notorious for his policies of "divide and rule", wherever he was posted, including Uganda. Internecine clashes between ethnic groups manifested themselves at the time of independence and beyond, can be partly attributed to this agitation.

The Belgian version of indirect rule in Rwanda and Burundi, encouraged animosity between the ruling class of minority Tutsi against the majority Hutu, by inculcating the notion among the Tutsi, that they were superior to the Hutu. The bad blood between the otherwise culturally and linguistically similar groups formed the building blocks for the Rwandan massacres of 1959, the Michel Micombero pogroms of 1972 in Burundi, and the mother of all terrors that culminated into the 1994 genocide in Rwanda.

Unlike the British, colonial powers from continental Europe, exercised direct rule. The French often appointed their own chiefs, based on their fidelity to the colonial administrators, sidelining hereditary leaders and other chieftains. There was no attempt at preserving African institutions which tended to compartmentalize people along tribal lines. Paris divided its territories into French West Africa, and Equatorial Africa, assigning a governor for each region. All laws governing these regions were formulated in Paris, but the system allowed French colonies to work together beyond the confines of ethnicities. The centralized nature of French rule forced universal interaction and subjugation to all, limiting rivalries and animosity between ethnic groups as prevailed under British rule.

The Portuguese practiced a harsher version of direct rule and seemed unwilling to loosen their grip on their African territories. When African countries began agitating for independence, the Portuguese dug-in, by declaring their African colonies as integral parts of Portugal. The Portuguese dictator Antonio de Oliveira Salazar who ruled Portugal from 1932-1968, went as far as declaring that Portugal and her colonies were one state, one territory, one citizenry and one government. However, Salazar's romanticization of Portuguese rule was not well received by the bulk of the oppressed people in the colonies. Independence in Portuguese colonies such as Mozambique and Angola came into being after long and protracted wars that left lasting physical and psychological effects on the populace.

In South Africa, the whites under the apartheid system, viewed Africans as permanently inferior to the extent of always needing guardianship. Germany as a colonial power didn't stay long enough in Africa. They only ruled from the 1880's until the Treaty of Versailles in 1919, following their defeat in WWI. But wherever they had ruled, they left a history of brutal treatment of their subjects. In Southwest Africa (Namibia), and Tanganyika (Tanzania) large farms were established, and the Germans used forced labor, crushing with maximum brutality and precision, any semblance of resistance. During Tanganyika's Maji Maji rebellion of 1905-8, an estimated 120,000 locals perished, setting off an outcry in many circles, that forced the Germans to implement some reforms. Subsequently, they formulated a policy called "scientific colonialism", under which they sought to convince their subjects, that German colonialism meant well. It was during this period that they undertook major capital projects such as the construction of the Dar-es-Salaam-Tabora railway. Then came WWI in 1914, in which Germany was the perpetrator, and lost the war and its possessions in 1918.

CHAPTER 4

Company rule was epitomized by Belgium's King Leopold II's approach in the Congo Free State (now Democratic Republic of Congo). He gave free rein to businessmen to maximize the exploitation of Congo's natural resources and transfer wealth to Belgium at any cost. Forced labor and the worst forms of brutality such as chopping off resistors' hands and ears were exercised with impunity. The Catholic Church played collaborator by running missionary schools that emphasized religious issues and nothing more. The missionary schools taught the Congolese how to become literate, albeit without the power of analysis.

Education in the Congo was structured to allow natives to read religious material without necessarily comprehending it. Another purpose was to create a reservoir of low-caliber citizens who could take instructions to aid colonialists as clerks. The Congo is by far the most staunchly catholic country on the continent. By the time the Belgians were forced to leave in a hurry after being coerced to grant independence in 1960, the country had as many as 600 priests, but only one college graduate. The country was by far, the least prepared to govern itself at independence, a trait that has nagged the country to this day. This has left the Congo poor and vulnerable to foreign exploitation, despite being easily one of the most natural resource endowed countries in the world.

The British also exercised indirect company rule under the auspices of the maverick entrepreneur Cecil Rhodes, (for whom the famous Rhodes scholarships at Oxford University in Britain are named). He set out in 1885 with a single-minded purpose of expanding the British territory in Africa, from Cape Town to Cairo. Within a period of only ten years, he managed to control the world's largest diamond mines in South Africa. He also attached his name to two vast territories which he called Southern and Northern Rhodesia (Zimbabwe and Zambia, respectively), controlled Nyasaland, (Malawi), and Bechuanaland (Botswana), all the while preventing the Boers under Paul Kruger, from extending their voortrekker migrations further north.

Cecil Rhodes engaged in a combination of intrigue, brinkmanship and trickery to achieve his goals in Africa. After his incredible success in mining in South Africa, he sought to duplicate this experience in areas further north, as part of his goal of expanding British colonial territory. In his quest, he negotiated and landed perhaps, one of the most lope-sided deals ever signed during the British colonial period.

Rhodes sent his business partner, named Charles Rudd, to meet and negotiate with Chief Lobengula of the Ndebele people of present-day Zimbabwe, for mineral rights. Prompted by a sense of urgency to thwart other interested advancing parties from getting to the chief before him, Rhodes tricked the chief into believing that he was only interested in the minerals, and not acquiring the land itself. Through bribery of some of his courtiers, and collaboration of a trusted British missionary, Rudd convinced the illiterate king to sign what came to be known as the Rudd Concession.

For this concession, the chief was promised 100 British pounds a month, 1,000 Martini Henry rifles, and 100,000 rounds of ammunition. But even these had a caveat attached. The first 500 rifles and 40,000 rounds of ammunition were to be delivered almost immediately, but the remainder would come after Rhodes had started his mining operations. Lobengula, to his detriment, also allowed Rhodes to place an armed steamer on the Zambezi, which would later be used to quell any revolts by the natives opposed to these intruders. And for precious little, the chief granted Rhodes and his party, the complete and exclusive rights to all minerals in his territory, including the power to defend these rights, and deny them to anyone else that might attempt to acquire them.

With this agreement secured, Rhodes set up a company he called the British South African Company and applied for a royal charter. The charter allowed him to administer a wide area that comprises the present-day Zimbabwe, Zambia and Malawi. On September 12,1890, Rhodes and his men hoisted the Union Jack in a small town they named Salisbury (Zimbabwe's capital Harare), and soon, white settlers began to arrive, seizing vast chunks of land from natives. Realizing that he had been tricked, Lobengula and his men launched an attack against the settlers in 1893, which was quashed. The Ndebele later attempted to push against the settlers by collaborating with their traditional archenemies, the Shona, in a united front that launched a major rebellion between 1896-97. This too, was badly crushed, paving the way for establishing the area as a British crown territory.

From 1890 to 1923, Rhodes' British South African Company administered this territory using the British model of indirect rule. After 1923, the Rhodesian colony became self-governing, with whites dominating almost all social and economic fabrics, akin to their neighbors to the south. There were even some attempts to create a loose federation which didn't materialize. Avenging for Cecil Rhodes' transgressions against Chief Lobengula must have been at the back of Comrade Robert Mugabe's mind when he seized white farmers' land to return it to its original owners.

CHAPTER 5

S ibling rivalry is as old as mankind itself. In the Book of Genesis, (25:19-34), we learn about how Isaac and Rebekah his wife first struggled and prayed to God to grant them a child. When their prayers were finally answered, Rebekah conceived. But during her pregnancy, the children jostled in the womb, leading her to ask the Lord why this was happening to her.

"Two nations are in your womb", the Lord told her.

"And two peoples from within you will be separated. One people will be stronger than the other, and the older will serve the younger".

Rebekah begat Isaac the twins Esau and Jacob. At birth, Esau the firstborn's body was like a hairy garment, and grew up to be a good hunter. He became his father's favorite child because Isaac had good taste for wild game. As the younger of the twins came out, he was grasping his brother's heel, as if to pull him back into the womb. They named him Jacob. He became his mother's favorite, and she showered him with love. It is said, that one day, Esau returned from a hunting trip quite famished and begged his brother for a bowl of lentil soup (red pottage). Jacob agreed to provide the soup, on condition that Esau would surrender to him his birthright (bekorah), to which Esau agreed.

Isaac was a man of advanced age when the twins were born, and, like all things old, his eyesight was failing him. His favorite son Esau had grown into a muscular and hairy young man whose arms he used to hold and stroke. All this happened in the glare presence of Rebekah, who was a keen observer of her husband.

One day, Isaac called his firstborn son Esau to his bedside, and said to him,

"My son, I am getting old, and I don't know when the Lord will call me from this world".

Esau listened attentively as his father continued,

"You know I like the taste of wild game, so I want you to take your bow and quiver of arrows, go to the field, bring your kill and prepare me my favorite dish, before I bestow upon you my blessing".

Esau followed his father's instructions, and left home for the hunt. But his mother Rebekah had overheard the conversation between Esau and his father and hatched a plan to have the blessing bestowed on her younger son Jacob.

So, while Esau was out hunting, Rebekah called Jacob, and told him about what the father had promised his elder brother and briefed him on a plan to sabotage it.

"Go get a goat from our herd", she instructed him, "then I'll prepare your father his favorite stew, which you can take him and secure the blessing".

"But my father will touch my body while blessing me, and you know Esau's is covered with a lot of hair", Jacob told his mother hesitatingly.

"Get the goat and leave the rest of the arrangements to me", Rebekah told her son.

Once the meat was ready, and the bread baked, Rebekah dressed Jacob in Esau's clothing and covered the arms and neck with goatskin, so that the younger man would feel like his brother.

Jacob took the meal to his father's bed and invited him to sit down and eat.

"My son, how did you get the game so quickly?", Isaac asked.

"Father, the Lord put the animal in my path", Jacob answered.

After the meal, Isaac asked his son to get closer, so he could receive his blessing.

"Are you Esau my firstborn?", the old man inquired one more time.

"Yes, my father", Jacob replied in a quivering voice. Then Isaac reached out and touched his arms and neck.

"The voice sounds like Jacob, but the arms and neck are Esau's". The ragged smell of Esau's clothing which his mother had given him, further satisfied Isaac, that this was indeed Esau. He put his hand on his son's head and bestowed a father's blessing as his own father Abraham had done to him.

Soon after, Esau came home with the hunt, prepared his father's favorite dish and took it to his father for the promised blessing. He woke up the old man and told him to sit and enjoy his meal before giving him the blessing.

"But I already gave you the blessing", said Isaac. It was at this point that both Isaac and Esau realized that Jacob had betrayed his brother and secured the blessing for himself.

"But can't you give me another blessing?", asked Esau in exasperation.

"No, this blessing can't be reversed once bestowed", Isaac said.

"I have made Jacob your master, and all his brothers shall be his servants", Isaac further told a broken and crest-fallen Esau.

In his anger, Esau vowed to kill his brother. But Rebekah heard about it and sent her younger son to live with her brother Laban in Haran until Esau's anger dissipated. Thereafter, the two continued to live apart, and formed two nations with different people.

In Abraham's patriarchal society, the birthright entitled the firstborn to the leadership of the family, and the judicial authority passed on by the father. By his impulsive action of trading his birthright for a bowl of soup, Esau showed that he didn't value the birthright, and was therefore not worthy of being the chosen one to continue shouldering responsibilities in the house of Isaac. Now he had lost the blessing to his younger brother too, and he was destined to remain Jacob's servant.

CHAPTER 6

Nearly 2,300 miles away in Kenya, and separated by more than three millennia, two Masai siblings would also enter a rivalry that would alter the course of their nation. Chief Lenana (name anglicized from the Masai Olonana), was born in 1870, to an influential Masai paramount tribal chief known as Mbatian, at Ngoshua, near Monduli around the foothills of Mount Kilimanjaro. His mother was one of Chief Mbatian's perhaps, 100 wives. And, although Lenana was born in a family of many children, he was an only son to his mother, and became one of his father's favorites, in a traditional society that put a premium on male children.

After the 2007 elections that saw Kenyans riot into the most violent political saga since independence, which claimed more than 1,000 lives, most analysts brushed it off as an inter-generational rivalry between Uhuru Kenyatta and his nemesis Raila Odinga. Afterall, it had happened before in the 1960's, when their fathers, Mzee Jomo Kenyatta, and Jaramoji Ojinga Odinga, one-time comrades in arms, turned bitter enemies soon after Kenya obtained its independence.

Prior to the elections, in 2005, an article was published in the East

African Newspaper, following the murder of a young and promising lawyer named Elijah Marima Sempeta. The article alluded to rare documents that Sempeta had painstakingly researched and obtained from London archives. The documents implicated both the British and Kenyan governments regarding the loss of vast land tracts the Maasai held in the early 1900's, during Chief Lenana's reign over the Masai.

Sempeta's probe started by questioning the monopoly of Magadi Soda Company (now renamed Tata Chemicals), over Lake Magadi soda ash. The lake's 222,788 acres happens to be part of land taken from the Maasai people. During his research, he had obtained copies of a 99-year lease that then Kenyan Governor Edward William Macleay Grigg had handed to the company in 1924. According to the document, this lease was good until 2023, so long as the company paid an annual fee of Ksh20 (equivalent to US 29 cents). To Sempeta, this appeared unconscionable that a company reputed to be Africa's largest soda ash producer, should have been paying so little for over 80 years.

Sempeta was not swayed by then company CEO, James Mathenge's argument that, besides the lease fee, the company had been paying millions of shillings in royalties to the Kenyan government and Olkajuedo County. In an act of bravado, the soft-spoken Sempeta and a group of other activists registered a company called Maa Resources Company, for the purpose of exploiting Soda ash from Lake Magadi for industrial uses by the community. The activists also added another twist, arguing that, since the Anglo-Maasai agreement of 1904 had expired in 2004, it was time for the remnants of the colonial order, and the government, to return those lands they occupied around Laikipia, to the original owners, the Maasai.

Sadly, Sempeta could not fulfill this dream, because his life was cut short by an assassin's bullet on March 9, 2005, near his home in Ngong town. Nevertheless, his dream had not been buried with him, because what he had uncovered with his research helped paint a clearer picture of pre-colonial land ownership in Kenya, especially in the Rift Valley area. Apart from the fact that most areas in the region still bear Maasai names, other evidence, including books and folklore, indicate that most of the current occupants (Kikuyu, Kalenjin, Kisii, Luhya, etc) came to the area after the Maasai were removed.

The Maasai vast lands extended from the foothills of Mt. Kilimanjaro in Tanzania, to the Baringo and Laikipia areas of the Rift Valley in western Kenya. This allowed them to exercise what one writer called rational grazing, which involved moving their herds to wet lowlands in the rainy season, and to higher ground during the drought.

Chief Mbatian, occupied a special place in the Maasai community. He was a Laibon, a position akin to a prophet, upon whom the wealth of the community depended due to his wisdom and forecasts of the future. He was a descendant of the great Inkindongi, a man associated with prophetic powers, who wandered and got lost in the Ngong area around 1640, and got rescued by a herdsman, according to Maasai folklore. In Maasai society, a Laibon can pass-on his prophetic powers to his heir. The traditions allowed a Laibon to accumulate a lot of wealth in form of cattle, and to marry as many wives as he wished without paying bride price. This created a lot of rivalry among the male children, sometimes engaging in innuendos against one another, in a feat to impress an aging father they wished to replace.

Chief Mbatian had an older son named Senteu from another wife, who was his favorite, and whom he was grooming to become Laibon after his death. But Lenana, who was his mother's only son, was couched by her to always be alert and on his feet so he could outmaneuver his elder brother. The two siblings started their subtle rivalry early in life, with each one trying everything he could to impress their aging father.

Lenana's circumcision and initiation rites had been delayed by his father due to the latter's involvement in Maasai tribal wars that lasted from 1830 to 1880. Once initiated, he became an apprentice prophet, because in the Maasai culture, the prophecy could be inherited. However, his future as a Laibon remained untenable, since Chief Mbatian preferred bestowing these powers on his favorite son, Senteu. So, while Mbatian allowed Senteu to interact with his clients to sharpen his skills, Lenana took to observing his father's operations, and in time, began to acquire his own clients and influence.

Mbatian himself had a cousin called Koikot who had challenged his legitimacy as a Laibon. This resulted into clashes that saw Koikot and his followers driven to Loroki plateau in Samburu. The defeat was so thorough that it left the vanquished without any cattle, resorting to hunting and gathering in order to survive. All this was happening before Lenana was initiated into manhood. By the time he was initiated at age 19, Mbatian's health was failing, and he had turned blind. He was thought to have been bewitched by another cousin called Makoo, since Maasai prophets didn't die of natural causes.

His failing health began causing a lot of anxiety, as he had not yet named a successor as Laibon. During this period, Lenana and Senteu's rivalry intensified, each attempting to gain favor from the father. Then, one day, as the chief lay on his deathbed, Lenana entered his manyatta and pretended to be Senteu, begging the old blind man to bestow his blessings upon him. The chief obliged, but soon after, Senteu, too, appeared for the same blessing. Unfortunately, Senteu was told, the blessing could not be reversed, and that Lenana was now the legitimate Laibon. From this point on, the brothers' rancor would spill-over into the public arena, and the British would exploit it, much to the detriment of the population they were about to colonize.

Chief Mbatian's death in 1890 coincided with the arrival of white settlers who were keen on capturing the vast Maasai lands in the Kenyan rift valley and highlands. Now in control, Lenana's power was constantly under threat from his disgruntled brother. By 1894, barely four years into his reign, Senteu, now living around Loita Hills, launched an attack on the Ilmatapato and Ilkaptutiei clans living around Nairobi, capturing large herds of cattle. This was followed soon after, by Kikuyu tribesmen, leaving Lenana with a traumatized community, devasted by hunger, and exhausted by war. Other events such as the drought of 1894-97, known as emutai, killed cattle by the thousands, and further exacerbated the situation. A rinderpest epidemic in 1899 nearly wiped out the community's cattle herds.

As the unending battles with his brother ensued, while he simultaneously battled other tribes, and sometimes launched restocking wars of his own, Lenana approached Francis Hall, an agent of the Imperial British East African company (IBEA), with a fort at Kabete for help. Hall saw an opening that would give his company, and by extension, British colonialists both an ally and opportunity to vanquish the Kikuyu and other tribes for their territorial expansion. The two sides found commonality in the old Chinese adage, "the enemy of my enemy is my friend", and saw friendship blossom between Lenana and Hall, resulting into his enthronement as Chief by the British Government in December 1898. Three years prior to this date, IBEA had ceded its territory to the British Government, although company officials remained behind, supervised by the Colonial office in London.

Lenana's recognition by the British was partly instigated by a desire to have someone they could supervise and control. At the time, Maasai domain covered territory that straddled over areas in present day Kenya and Tanzania. And, Lenana's pursuit of his brother's warriors sometimes spilled over into Tanganyika, causing a diplomatic row, since the latter was, at the time, under German control. Once in their camp, the British appointed Sydney Langford Hinde as a resident political agent to the Maasai Agency. His role was essentially to persuade Lenana and win him over through bogus offers for Maasai land concessions. He succeeded in doing this and then some.

With Lenana contained, the British turned their focus on his brother Senteu, whose warriors operated from bases near Mt. Kilimanjaro in Tanganyika. By 1902, the pressure exerted on him, coupled with a string of other setbacks forced Senteu out of Tanganyika, to seek a truce with the British, thereby clearing all obstacles to the Maasai land takeover in Kenya. Thereafter, in two major controversial land concessions signed by Chief Lenana, one in 1904, and the other in 1911, referred to as "the tragedy of the commons", the chief literally handed over Maasai land to the colonial British settlers.

The colonial settlers whose numbers began to swell around 1902, set their eyes on the Kenya highlands and Rift Valley areas, which they considered more suitable for raising livestock. They also considered this land unoccupied, since the nomadic Maasai usually moved away seasonally with their cattle in search of better pasture.

The Uganda railway, which run through this land was vulnerable to attacks by the Nandi, who occupied the plateau to the west of the

Mau escarpment. Their leader, Chief Koitalel arap Samoei repeatedly attacked the railway and telegraph lines, until the British had had enough with him. In September 1905, a military operation was sent in to put him out of action, vanquishing the community, and confining it into a reserve by 1906.

Charles Elliot, a colonial administrator went as far as arguing in the Devonshire White paper that justified the massive land-grabbing, saying,

"I cannot admit that wandering tribes have a right to keep other and superior races out of large tracts merely because they have acquired a habit of straggling over far more land than they can utilize."

Most settlers from Britain and South Africa who applied to the colonial office for land in the Rift Valley area, always got it. By the end of 1905, over one million acres of land had been either leased or sold to various groups of settlers. Among the largest applicants were a South African company called The East African Syndicate, which acquired 320,000 acres in the Naivasha District in 1904. The other big landlord was Lord Delamere, who initially wanted 100,000 acres of the Maasai's best grazing land between lakes Nakuru and Naivasha. Although his application for this particular spot was turned down, he was allocated another chunk of land on the Molo River.

Sources, including Encyclopedia Britannica, point out that these allocations did not go on without Maasai objections. At first, Elliot appeared to listen to the Maasai chiefs and elders, stopping the process for a little while. However, when he resigned his position, his successor, Donald Stewart, immediately summoned Maasai chiefs, including Lenana, Masikondi and Legalishu, representing the Purko, Kakonyuke, Loita, Damat and L'Otayok clans. This happened on August 9, 1904. Stewart gave the chiefs the option of freely moving their communities to other lands the government was offering them or be forced to move out of the Rift Valley anyway. Following that meeting, Stewart produced a document, purported to be "an agreement", which the chiefs signed. The agreement stipulated that the Maasai were bound to this agreement so long as the Maasai shall exist as a race. As soon as the lands in Kinangop Plateau, Kedong and greater Gilgil were allocated, the Masaai were entirely removed from the Rift Valley, and settled in Laikipia Plateau, at the time occupied by the Laikipiak clan.

The uprooting of the Maasai from the Rift Valley marked the beginning of Kenya's land wrangles which persist up to now. When Kenya started agitating for independence, among the major issues of the day, was the return of those lands to their original owners. But when independence finally came, and most settlers left the country, land ownership in the Rift Valley and Kenya highlands did not revert to the original owners. Instead, the new ruling class of politicians wantonly took over thousands of the best farmland acreage, sometimes ruthlessly evicting the poor tenants who had encroached on the edges of the vast estates. It's this new class of "settlers", now controlling the country's military and legal apparatus, who sponsored armed groups to run amok, and chase out the undesirable elements who were trying to reclaim their ancestral land in the Rift Valley. This, in essence, was the cause of the 2008 riots in Kenya, which resulted in a loss of over one thousand lives.

While Chief Lenana was a strong and powerful man who held sway with many chiefs and elders in the Maasai community, the British valued him. They even paid him a salary and counted him as an ally who could subdue rebellious communities. But once he acceded to the concessions that would perpetually remove the Maasai from their ancestral land, he outlived his usefulness and became disposable. This was evident in 1911, when the chief contracted a severe case of dysentery that soon ended his life. Rather than take him to a hospital in Nairobi, only 16 kilometers from his home at Kiserian, the colonial officials preferred to monitor him from a safe distance.

After succumbing to his ailment, the same officials rushed in to view his emaciated body. Even then Governor of Kenya, Girouard Percy showed up, showering the fallen chief with praises, and reminding his people to honor his wishes, at the top of which was, (allegedly), that the Maasai should leave Laikipia to the white settlers.

However, with a twist of irony about a chief who was left to die under deplorable and preventable circumstances by his erstwhile handlers, someone must have appreciated the services he rendered to the white settlers with his concessions over Maasai lands. Chief Lenana's spirit continues to soar higher than those of his compatriots, literally and figuratively. His name will forever, be perched on Mt Kenya's third highest peak, now known as Lenana Peak (16,355 ft) above sea level. The highest peak on Mt. Kenya (17,057 ft), is named for his father, Chief Mbatian.

Mt Kenya is Africa's second tallest mountain, only dwarfed by Mt Kilimanjaro, whose Kibo Peak (19,341 ft) forms the roof of the Continent and lies about 200 miles to the south.

CHAPTER 7

I t's an old cliché, that power is never surrendered freely. It must be fought for and wrested from those who hold it. The Maasai were not the only Kenyan ethnic community robbed and dispossessed of their land by white settlers. The Mau Mau Rebellion, which was fought between 1952 and 1960, against the British Colonial government, was organized, and drew its fighting force, mainly from aggrieved Kikuyu, the numerically largest tribal group in Kenya at the time.

The rebellion was by far, the most significant event that precipitated and hastened the end of British rule in Kenya. Its origins were rooted in issues concerning displacement of the Kikuyu from their ancestral land, suppression of their rights, including free movement, arbitrary arrests, poor representation on national issues, and poverty. For decades since white settlement reached its peak in the 1930's Kikuyu community leaders had been demanding that the colonial government return land seized from their people, and they were continually ignored. By 1945, the Kenya African Union (KAU), led by Jomo Kenyatta, had taken the mantle to demand the return of the Kikuyu land, but they, too, were ignored.

Realizing the futility of their mission, a splinter and more radical group emerged from recruiting members from equally affected tribes such as Embu and Meru, to attack opponents of the military approach, and to raid settlers' farms, including the destruction of livestock. The Mau Mau fighters were bound together by an oath of secrecy regarding their mission. However, the insurgency took a different turn after the colonial government declared a state of emergency in October 1952, allowing the British government to ship in army reinforcements.

Many local communities were shattered as men and women were arbitrarily arrested and interned in camps far away from their villages, akin to the American Japanese internment following the Japanese bombing of Pearl Harbor. Others, suspected to be Mau Mau guerillas were summarily hanged, or shot execution style. Yet the insurgency dragged on, with determined fighters setting bases in the extensive forests of Mt. Kenya, and surrounding areas, occasionally launching attacks in major cities like Nairobi, Nakuru and Mombasa. The army, in return, conducted many brutal acts on those suspected to be collaborators with the insurgents. Whatever bad acts they couldn't do themselves, they recruited home guards, who went on a rampage, terrorizing suspicious communities, destroying properties, and crops, at times leaving whole communities on the verge of starvation.

The casualties of the Mau Mau insurgency were many on both sides of the political divide. The officials of the colonial administration put the death toll at 11,000 people, including 1,090 fighters convicted and hanged. The figure reported for white settlers was only 32 for the entire eight years of the revolt. The Kenyan Human Rights Commission has put the number of those executed, maimed and tortured as high as 90,000, with an additional 160,000 incarcerated in appalling and degrading circumstances.

Professor David Anderson, a leading expert on African politics at Oxford University, has estimated the death toll at 25,000.

Whatever the true figure of casualties was, the fact remains that the suppression of the Mau Mau Rebellion in Kenya was one of the worst cases of brute force used by the British during their long colonial history.

The Home Guard, drawn from rival tribes, and cooperating

members of the Kikuyu tribe itself, were trained and armed by the colonial administration, to spy, raid, and arrest suspected members of the insurgency, as a way of controlling the population. The property of a suspected insurgent, including home and farm products, could be pillaged, at will, and the owner killed or maimed with impunity.

Some of the indiscretions, humiliations and betrayals during the Mau Mau rebellion are well dramatized in Ngugi wa Thiongo's book, titled "A Grain of Wheat". In one scene, he depicts Gikonyo, a popular local carpenter, whose workshop had become a meeting place for Kikuyu men from Thabai village. These men were among the multitudes who had taken the Mau Mau oath to join the resistance during the National Emergency declared by the colonial regime.

Among those who were a frequent presence at Gikonyo's workshop, was Karanja, a boyhood friend of Gikonyo. Good at his craftmanship with his tools, despite his low-key approach, Gikonyo had even managed to win over the heart of a local beauty called Mumbi, much to the chagrin of more flamboyant suitors who sought Mumbi's hand.

The couple were living happily together, along with Gikonyo's mother Wangari, until one morning, the Home Guard came and snatched him from his hut while Mumbi and Wangari were out attending to their chores. Gikonyo was hauled first, to Yali camp, then from detention camp to detention camp, where men could be seriously beaten up or even hanged for making disparaging remarks about the white man's oppressive regime. Most days were spent in hard labor quarries, gathering stones used to build elaborate and fortified residences for the oppressor.

These men were sworn to secrecy under the oath and were highly disciplined. The warders who oversaw the detainees' work in the field discouraged loose talk about the emergency, particularly words that were deemed to cause further hatred for the regime. Those who were caught violating this rule, were severely punished with beatings, starvation, solitary confinement, and in extreme cases, hanged indiscreetly, to paint the picture of a suicide, as happened to one talkative fellow detainee named Gatu.

But human endurance can sometimes be stretched to a limit, and beyond certain conditions, even men of a steely character, have been known to succumb. The suppressors of the rebellion applied the kind of pressure aimed at breaking men on edge, to yield and confess to them who was in the resistance, so that more arrests could be made. However, once they crumbled, they were quickly given incentives to join the home guards, becoming part of the oppressor. Karanja had been such a man. It was even thought that he had everything to do with Gikonyo's detention.

The day Gatu was picked up from the quarry by the guards, and his body later found dangling in his cell, he had just poured out his heart to Gikonyo about how his life had become meaningless after another man snatched and married his intended bride. Gikonyo was not only touched by Gatu's story but was later devastated by his death. In his own mind, he kept wondering if Mumbi would wait for him to return from detention, if he survived it, or would also end up in the arms of another man. After agonizing over it all night long, Gikonyo had, early morning, decided to turn himself in to the guards so that he could go back home to be with his beloved Mumbi.

It had been six years since his arrest, and upon his release from camp, Gikonyo staggered through abandoned villages, and terrain that had been completely changed due to land consolidation. First, he could not even find the location of his mother's hut, where both Mumbi and Wangari lived. But, after asking for directions from rather indifferent men and women, who mainly looked away, or simply stared at this shabby-looking man with a torn hat he'd picked from the road, a young boy led him to his mother hut.

Finding the simple wooden door open, he hesitates about entering the smoke-filled hut, as if something hideous is inside, and instead raises his voice to inquire if anybody was there. Mumbi hears the voice and emerges to find Gikonyo at the door. Her mouth goes agape, as she steps back, partly in amazement, but also to let him in. Some lump is choking his throat as he stares at Mumbi with a young infant strapped tightly on her back. It is quite clear this is not his child. Wangari hears her son's voice and comes staggering to embrace him. But his arms are in no mood to touch anyone. He asks to sit down and leans against one of the poles supporting the hut, and simply stares at the roof.

Finally, he asks Mumbi the inevitable question,

"Whose child, is it?"

Mumbi chokes on the answer, until Wangari comes to the rescue.

"Karanja!"

"Karanja, my friend?", Gikonyo asks rhetorically, not expecting an answer.

"Mumbi waited so long for you my son, these things happen", Wangari cut him short.

An immediate sinister thought crossed Gikonyo's mind, to eliminate both Mumbi and the child from this haunting scene.

But first, he must report to the chief of the home guards as part of the conditions given to him upon release, for rehabilitation into the community.

He asks for directions to the chief's office, and once he gets there, he knocks at the half-open door. A voice beckons him to enter, but his mind is elsewhere, so he knocks again.

"I said come in", the man inside raises his voice a notch higher, as he watches Gikonyo walk in.

"Sit down", commands the man behind the desk, as Gikonyo finally realizes that the chief is none other than Karanja. This is the same man who used to play a guitar with him, spent endless hours in his workshop, took the oath with him, and for all that, he paid him back by fathering a child with his wife in his absence.

Gikonyo makes a dash towards Karanja's throat, but the latter draws a pistol and orders him to sit down. When Gikonyo refuses to obey the order, Karanja points to the watch tower outside, and says,

"The rules have changed for those who rebel against the white man", he said.

"You either cooperate, or we'll keep you in that tower for a long time!"

However, despite Karanja's stern warnings, Gikonyo stormed out, determined to get rid of Mumbi and her child. He rushed to Wangari's hut hoping to find Mumbi and her child there, but the door was locked. At first, he thought they had locked themselves inside, having failed to notice the sisal rope that tied it to one of the roof supports from outside. So, with all his force, he pushed against the wooden door, but it wouldn't yield. Then, like someone possessed, he took a few steps back, and then came charging at the structure, which separated from its frame, and crushed to the floor inside. Gikonyo crushed with it, hitting his head against the grindstone, and laid on the ground unconscious, foaming at the mouth.

Such atrocities and indignities were mainly swept under the rug when the British turned over power to Kenyans at Independence on December 12, 1963. However, the pain never went away, especially for those families which were directly impacted. So, when in 2009, the London Law firm of Leigh Day & Co, opened a case on behalf of five individuals who were directly tortured by the British, the government in London argued that its culpability could be excused by the long passage of time. Moreover, they said, responsibility now rests with the Kenyan government which took over from them.

But with a lot of pressure and condemnation bearing on the British government, they finally relented, and the families were awarded a sum of 20 million pounds for their suffering, although one of the plaintiffs died before the case was settled.

One outspoken Conservative Member of Parliament, Enoch Powell, called the suppression exercise, "a river of blood", and that if those who conducted it could go unpunished, then the British didn't deserve an empire.

CHAPTER 8

Uganda experienced a relatively smoother relationship under the British colonial administration than Kenya. Despite all its fertile and well-watered virgin territory, the British did not attempt to grab some of it the same way they did in Kenya, or Zimbabwe (Southern Rhodesia). Among the reasons usually given were that both Kabaka Mutesa I, who invited the Europeans, and later, his son Mwanga, were so adamant against foreign entities touching "the people's land". Another plausible reason is that the British had such a small community which would not have provided them the security needed outside Kampala. Most of the Europeans in the country resided in the Kampala/Entebbe area. But for Uganda, these reasons are not quite convincing, given that local chiefs and whole communities in other colonies were equally strongly opposed to occupation. Moreover, the British had the military wherewithal to accomplish the forceful occupation had they chosen to do so.

The first Englishman to enter Buganda Kingdom was John Hanning Speke, who arrived in 1862. Arab traders from Zanzibar had preceded him in the 1840's, in search of ivory and slaves. But it was the British-

American explorer Henry Morton Stanley, who met Kabaka Mutesa I in 1875, and persuaded him to allow British missionaries to come to his territory. Morton Stanley had arrived at the Kabaka's Court at Rubaga, only to find that the Arabs were already flirting to convert the king to Islam, after showering him with gifts.

During his short stay, Stanley had been impressed with the Kabaka's enlightenment on many issues, including organization, attire, standing army, and local roads known as "bulungi bwansi.", not to mention the Kiganda culture, which he found intriguing. Endowed with a lush green vegetation, mild climate and abundant natural resources, Stanley had called it "the Pearl of Africa", a phrase later popularized by Winston Churchill after visiting the country at the beginning of the 20th century. Stanley laid down a proposal for the Kabaka, in which the British would send in missionaries, educators and technicians to help him develop his kingdom. But the Kabaka, suspicious of foreigners' intentions, decided to accommodate both the Arabs and Europeans, exploiting their rivalries, and marking the beginning of the spread of foreign religions in the country.

It was during his stay at the Kabaka's court at Rubaga, that Colonel Ernest Linant de Bellefonds, son of French Engineer Louis Maurice Linant de Bellefonds, who was involved in the construction of the Suez Canal, joined him. He had been sent as an emissary of Emin Pasha, then Administrator of Anglo-Egyptian Sudan at its Equatoria Headquarters.

Stanley drafted the proposal, handed it to Colonel Linant, and proceeded with his mission of circumnavigating Lake Victoria and its surroundings. However, on his way back to Egypt, the Colonel, who was escorted by a contingent of Nubian soldiers, was attacked by Bari tribesmen at Laboreh on August 26, 1875, and Linant was among those killed. The Bari were avenging the Nubians for their cooperation and participation with slave raiders. The colonel's body was left out to rot by the riverbank. By sheer luck, Stanley's blood-stained letter was recovered from one of the boots worn by the slain colonel, forwarded to General Gordon in Khartoum, who forwarded it to London, where it was published in the Daily Telegraph to revving reviews. In the letter, Stanley admonished the British government to take advantage of the enlightened Kabaka Mutesa who controlled a large territory of immense wealth and beauty.

The letter spurred a lot of interest about Uganda, not only in Britain, but even beyond, prompting the British to take some action. The anti-slavery movement urged the British government to urgently introduce Christianity in order to halt the spread of Islam. Two years after the letter's publication, the Church Missionary Society (CMS) dispatched its first missionaries to the country in 1877. Other European colonial powers also took interest, and by 1879, a French Catholic missionary expedition, led by Father Simeon Lourdel (later christened Father Mapera by locals, from the French mon père), accompanied by fellow Frenchman Brother Amans Delmas landed at Bugonga on the Entebbe Peninsula, having travelled from France via Zanzibar.

During the 25 years between 1875 when Morton Stanley first met Kabaka Mutesa I, and the signing of the Buganda Agreement on March 10, 1900, there were many upheavals in the country, following clashes between the British colonialists and various factions of local chiefs who were opposed to their presence. The most prominent opponent to British rule was Omukama (King) Kabalega of Bunyoro Kingdom. The kingdom of Bunyoro-Kitara had been established in the 15th century, and had become the most dominant in the region, extending from northwestern Uganda, to Karagwe, southwest of Lake Victoria in present day Tanzania. However, its rapid expansion became its own undoing, as smaller, more compact kingdoms like Buganda, took advantage of loosely controlled borders to expand their own territory.

The British took advantage of the rivalry between Kabaka Mutesa I of Buganda, and Omukama Kabalega of Bunyoro, rendering support to the Kabaka towards the weakening, and eventual defeat and exile of the recalcitrant Kabalega, all this in return for Mutesa's cooperation.

Kabalega was born on June 18, 1853, to Omukama Kamurasi Mirundi Rukanama rwa Kanembe Kyebambe IV of Bunyoro-Kitara. His mother went by the names Kanyange Nyamutahingurwa Omunyonzakati Abwooli. He was 16 years old when he took the Bunyoro-Kitara throne upon the death of his father in 1869, becoming the 23rd Omukama from the Babiito dynasty, and taking on the name

Chwa II. The young monarch immediately embarked on major tasks aimed at restoring the kingdom's glory, including reclaiming lost territory, increased food production, and trade in iron tools and salt.

He was described as an excellent war tactician, whose black smiths acquired the skill of duplicating European guns, including his famous "Bagwigairebata". It was such tactics he used to defeat Sir Samuel Baker in 1872 at Masindi, preventing the latter from annexing and adding Bunyoro Kingdom and Acholiland to the Equatorial region of Anglo-Egyptian Sudan. Kabalega formed alliances with other kings and chiefs opposed to British rule and continued to be a thorn in the colonial administration's flesh. In Buganda, his traditional enemies, he backed Prince Kalema against his brother Mwanga II, the reigning Kabaka, forcing the monarch to flee to Bulingugwe Island in Lake Victoria, where he stayed for a year.

During his "Nyangire" (I refused) revolt against the colonial onslaught on his kingdom, Kabalega crossed into Acholiland, and was hidden and protected by Chief Awich Abok of Payira. He co-opted fighters from Nubia and Somalia into his army to fight the British. But on April 9, 1899, Kabalega, who was by then allied with Mwanga II against the British, was caught after being shot and wounded. He was then exiled to the Seychelles Islands in the Indian Ocean where he spent 24 years before being allowed to return. However, on his way back, he died in the eastern Ugandan town of Jinja.

Omukama Kabalega is a celebrated figure in Uganda, the only person besides Queen Elizabeth II, for whom a national park (formerly Murchison Falls) is named. He was declared a national hero by President Yoweri Museveni in 2009.

Kabaka Danieri Bassamula Ekkere Mwanga II was born in 1866 to Kabaka Mutesa I and took the reign of the Buganda throne in 1884, at the tender age of 18, following his father's death. The Bassamula Ekkere (makes frogs croak), likely refers to the cruelty during his reign. Coincidentally, his enthronement happened the same year that the Berlin Conference took place, during which European Powers sought to allocate themselves vast territories of what was then referred to as the Dark continent. From the start, the young king had to balance the daily demands of his subjects, against the forces of intruding European and Arab powers, all of whom were attempting to court and influence him in competition with one another using Christianity and Islam.

Mwanga saw the foreign influences of converting his subjects into either Islam or Christianity, as a direct threat to his rule, since the converts tended to cast away the traditional beliefs which formed the base of the Kabaka's power. In October 1885, his order to Bishop James Hannington's captors in Busoga, resulted in the murder of the man of the cloth, over a Luganda phrase "bamutte" (release him), but which translates as "kill him" in the Lusoga language. Strong opposition to these foreign influences served as the backdrop to the Kabaka's order to burn alive, 45 Christian people of faith (now known as Uganda Martyrs) at Namugongo on June 3, 1886. Twenty-two of the mostly young adolescents belonged to the Catholic faith, while another twenty-three were Anglicans. On October 18, 1964, Pope Paul VI, canonized the 22 Abajulizi ba Uganda into the family of Catholic Saints, and in 1969, he traveled on a pilgrimage to Uganda, becoming the first reigning pontiff to visit sub-Saharan Africa.

However, instead of this grotesque action by the Kabaka limiting the spread of foreign religions, it created more cooperation between the converts and the missionaries, while rivalry among religious entities became fierce. The Catholics aligned themselves with the French, the Anglicans sided with the British, while the Moslems identified with the Arabs. As a result, the Kabaka grew more isolated, and his influence among his subjects continued to wane. After the execution of the Christian converts at Namugongo, the missionaries grew wary of his atrocities, and continued to undermine his authority. By 1897, he had joined his erstwhile rival, Omukama Kabalega of Bunyoro in opposition to colonial rule. The British bundled the two recalcitrant kings and exiled them to the Indian Ocean Island of Seychelles, where Mwanga died in 1903 aged 37 years. Mwanga II was succeeded by his young son Daudi Chwa II, in 1897, who reigned through Regents on account of his young age.

Rivalry among these religious faiths persists up to now, although

Uganda has been spared of the ominous violence that afflicted other countries in similar situations.

The Buganda Agreement was signed on the 10th of March 1900, between Sir Henry Hamilton Johnston, K.C.B, Her Majesty's Special Commissioner, Commander-in-Chief, and Consul-General of the Uganda Protectorate, on behalf of Her Majesty the Queen of Great Britain, on one hand, and the Regents and Chiefs on behalf of the Kabaka of Buganda. The main purpose of the agreement was to define a territorial entity called Buganda, which was the area under the control of the Kabaka. The area was mapped out using an old system of metes and bounds, characterized by listing compass bearings and distances of boundaries.

The survey curved out a total of 19,600 square miles, out of which, the two largest portions, one consisting of 8,000 sq. miles was allocated to 1,000 chiefs and private landowners, while another comprising of 9,000 sq. miles, popularly known as "Mayilo Kenda", was held in trust by Her Majesty the Queen's government and reserved for future generations. The Kabaka and his family, were allocated 350 sq. miles. Other significant allocations included 1,500 sq. miles for forests, 320 sq. miles allocated to the 20 Saza chiefs of the original 20 counties in Buganda, divided into 160 sq. miles for the chiefs's private use, and 160 sq. miles for county headquarters. Religious institutions were allocated 92 sq. miles, while the remainder was parceled out to key constituencies such as the Kabaka's relatives, and Regents, necessary for the smooth functioning of Obuganda.

In Uganda, there are four basic types of land tenure systems, namely,

(i) Customary land – predominantly practiced in the northern and eastern regions
(ii) Freehold system
(iii) Mailo land – a system common in Buganda
(iv) Leasehold system.

Under the customary land tenure system, the community owns the land, and its use may be determined by a chief or some other authority entrusted with the power to rule over such matters. Users normally do not hold titles to the parcels they occupy.

The freehold tenure system is the easiest to understand and operate, in that ownership is in perpetuity, and has a title, allowing for easy sale and transfer.

Mailo land tenure system traces its origins from the Buganda Agreement of 1900 between the Regents of the young Kabaka Daudi Chwa II, and representatives of the British colonial government. As noted above, the 19600 square miles of Buganda land, were parceled out and allocated to different entities in units based on a square mile, hence the title "Mailo land".

This system operates like freehold, allowing a title to be held in perpetuity, but unlike freehold, it also respects the rights of bona fide tenants, provided they pay "busuulu", or ground rent to the owner. There are two types of mailo land, official, which cannot be sold, but can accommodate tenants who pay busuulu to the Buganda kingdom, and private mailo land whose tenants pay the private landlord.

With the existence of two mailo land tenure systems in Buganda, ordinary citizens are not always sure how each one works. The bulk of the tenants who pay ground rent are on official mailo land managed by the Buganda Land Board (BLB). For most of the period since its inception at the beginning of the twentieth century, the system worked smoothly, partly because the population was relatively low. However, beginning in the 1980's, the population explosion started causing landless people to take the law into their own hands, sometimes invading absent landlords' parcels categorized as mailo land.

The situation wasn't helped by the BLB, which has sometimes taken advantage of the absent private mailo landowners and leased it out as if it was official mailo land. The Museveni government recently started cracking down on these illegal leases, with the Minister of lands going so far as announcing a cancelation of those leases. However, the private owners do not necessarily get their parcels back. Rather, the government prefers keeping those landless citizens on the occupied land, and instead promises to compensate the owners for the loss of their properties. The process has been criticized as a government seizure of private properties, whose compensation drags on for years, and in the majority of cases, has been prioritized based on the owner's assessed allegiance to the President's party, the National Resistance Movement (NRM).

Leasehold land not held by BLB, is mainly controlled by government or such agencies as cities, town councils or municipalities. These bodies control the lease terms and agreements under which this type of land is managed. The commonest leases are issued on 49-year or 99-year terms.

It is noteworthy, that while the colonial government reserved the right to undertake projects for the public good, it laid out a basis for compensating owners of the allocated lands, in case the government wished to undertake civil works such as the construction of roads, railways, tunnels, bridges, airports, etc. The agreement also stipulates a case for compensation over mineral rights in case a resource the government wished to exploit was located on private land. The concept under which a government or other authority such as a city or local council forcefully takes over an individual's or a community's land for purposes of erecting a structure such as a school, or constructing a road, is referred to as Eminent Domain.

The Uganda Protectorate was created in 1894, after the British Imperial East African Company ceded its territory to the British Government, the same way that Cecil Rhodes had transferred ownership of Rhodesia to the British. At the time of the Ugandan territory transfer, almost all this land consisted of the Kingdom of Buganda. More territory that constitutes the country known as Uganda today, would later be added after the Buganda Agreement of 1900, and, after finalizing negotiations with other kings and tribal leaders outside Buganda Kingdom.

CHAPTER 9

There are 54 countries in the African Union, out of which 46 are categorized as sub-Saharan. Except for a brief occupation by Italy from October 3, 1935, to February 19, 1937, Ethiopia remained the only sovereign state on the continent that was never colonized by a foreign power. All the rest have now obtained independence, the latest one being South Sudan, which broke away from Sudan on July 9, 2011.

Ghana (formerly known as Gold Coast) was the first sub-Saharan country to obtain independence from Britain on March 6, 1957. Until then, the country consisted of small independent kingdoms before and during colonial rule, which Kwame Nkrumah, the founding father, stringed together and consolidated into a republic when the country gained its independence. These kingdoms included Dagomba and Gonja in the north, Ashanti in the midlands, and the Fanti in the coastal region.

Kwame Nkrumah was born on September 21, 1909, in Nkroful, in what was then the British Colony of the Gold Coast. Raised as a Roman Catholic, he attended and spent the first nine years of his schooling at Half Assini, from where he proceeded to Achimota College. Graduating as a teacher at Achimota in 1930, he taught in junior Catholic schools in both Elmina and Axim, at one time, also teaching at a seminary. Five years later, he left teaching to further his studies in the United States, where he enrolled at Lincoln University, graduating in 1939. Later that same year, he entered the University of Pennsylvania to study for a Masters' degree.

It was while he attended U-Penn, that he immersed himself in the socialist ideas of Karl Marx, Vladimir Lenin, and influential black American activists of the 1920's such as Marcus Garvey. He organized student activities and was even elected President of the African Students Organization in the US and Canada. In May 1945, Nkrumah moved to England, where he organized the 5th Pan-African Congress in the midland city of Manchester. In 1947, Nkrumah returned home to serve as General Secretary of the United Gold Coast Convention (UGCC), which had been formed by J.B Danquah. But once Nkrumah toured the country, he concluded that the pressure to achieve independence would be more effective if the new party was run as a mass movement. This caused a rift between Danquah's elitist middle-class leaders, and the more radical approach preferred by Nkrumah's supporters. By 1949, Nkrumah's group had a new party called the Convention Peoples Party (CPP), a mass movement that agitated for immediate self-governance. In January 1950, the party embarked on a series of positive non-violent activities such as strikes and non-cooperation with the colonial government.

The CPP's strikes caused a lot of economic disruptions forcing the colonial government to arrest Nkrumah and sentence him to one year in jail. However, the election of February 8, 1951, demonstrated overwhelming support for Nkrumah and the CPP. Subsequently, the government released him from prison, and he became leader of government business in 1952, from which he advanced to the first Prime Minister of the Gold Coast.

The Gold Coast, together with the British Togoland Trust territory finally achieved independence from Britain on March 6, 1957, under its ancient name, Ghana. Initially, his popularity soared as the newly independent government embarked on extending more services by constructing new roads, schools, and hospitals. The popularity was further buttressed by the policy of Africanization which thrust indigenous Ghanaians into new roles previously reserved for white colonialists. Nevertheless, although he had been elected as a populist, Nkrumah's governing style soon became increasingly authoritarian.

After the 1960 plebiscite that turned Ghana into a republic, Nkrumah became an executive president with wide latitude and powers under the new constitution. The president took on large and ambitious projects that pushed the country's debt burden to unsustainable levels. Although some of the projects, like the Soviet-sponsored nuclear reactor at Kwabenya, whose foundation stone he laid on November 25, 1964, turned out to be white elephants, the speech he delivered on that occasion still evokes memories of what a visionary he was. In that speech, he admonished Ghanaians, and Africans as a whole, to embrace the benefits of research and technology, which would bring them at par with the more advanced societies of the time. He advocated for nuclear energy to be harnessed for peaceful purposes for its potential to provide cheap energy for industrial and domestic uses, even calling for an integrated energy system that combined nuclear, hydro and solar power, a revolutionary idea for the 1960's. His ideas of developing science clubs all over the country, to educate and interest ordinary people, if embraced and implemented, would have transformed Ghana in Kennedy-like fashion, when he challenged the US to embark on a project to send a man to the moon and return him to earth within a decade.

Unfortunately, Nkrumah's vision remained a pipe dream, as he kowtowed more with socialist policies. The executive presidency had given him more powers, some of which he used to settle scores and suppress opposition from his detractors. This took his attention away from domestic issues, and his popularity at home started waning. And the fact that Nkrumah flirted too much with socialism, didn't please western countries, especially former colonial power Britain. For that matter, Nkrumah had become a marked person.

As the economy began to deteriorate under heavy debt, Nkrumah ignored events at home, and instead turned his focus towards Pan-

Africanism, pushing an effort to liberate every country on the continent that was still under colonial domination. He also took up a personality cult, acquiring the title "Osagyefo", meaning "Redeemer" in the Akan language, this, after being declared "life president" for both his party and the nation. True to his ideals of Pan-Africanism, in 1958, he had married Helena Fathia Halim Ritzk, an Egyptian woman of the Coptic Faith, who became the First Lady of the newly independent nation of Ghana.

An attempted assassination over his life in August 1962, caused the once ebullient Nkrumah to be isolated from his people, choosing to be surrounded only by cronies he could trust. In 1964, he declared Ghana a one-party state, with himself at the apex. Meanwhile, the economy continued deteriorating, with shortages of basic consumables causing an escalation in prices. On February 24, 1966, while on a visit to Beijing, China, the army and police staged a coup d'état which removed him from power.

Nkrumah returned to West Africa after the coup, but not to Ghana. He lived in exile in Conakry, under protection by Guinean President, and fellow left-leaning Ahmed Sekou Toure. The Osagyefo died in 1972, while undergoing treatment for cancer in Bucharest, Romania, then ruled by communist dictator Nicolae Ceausescu, who himself got ousted, and was executed by a military firing squad, together with his wife, Elena, in December 1989, following the fall of communism.

Kwame Nkrumah was one of the founding fathers of the Organization of African Unity (OAU) in 1963, along with such other luminaries of the era as Emperor Haile Selassie of Ethiopia, Mzee Jomo Kenyatta of Kenya, Felix Houphouet-Boigny of Cote d'Ivoire, Leopold Senghor of Senegal, Mwalimu Julius Nyerere of Tanzania, Milton Obote of Uganda, and Kenneth Kaunda of Zambia. For that reason, Nkrumah remains a celebrated icon as a statesman on the African continent, nearly fifty years after his death.

For the next 13 years after Nkrumah's ouster, Ghana was plagued with a retinue of lackluster performing leaders whose priority appeared to be enriching themselves from state coffers, while neglecting the country's economy. This crippled the once thriving economy into shambles, turning it into a basket case. Then, in 1979, a young Flight-Lieutenant in the Ghanaian Airforce, named Jerry John Rawlings, together with other like-minded junior officers, tired of the mess and plunder by the country's leaders, led a military coup in which he was installed as Ghana's leader. During the short rule (112 days) of the Armed Forces Revolutionary Council, two former heads of state, General Ignatius Kutu Acheampong and Lt-Gen Frederick W. K Akuffo, were tried, found guilty by a military tribunal, and summarily executed in public view at the beach.

Jerry Rawlings handed over power to an elected civilian-led government under Hilla Limann. The new president sought to protect his position by retiring Rawlings. However, two years later, when the new president reverted to the same corruption the Rawlings group had tried to eliminate, the brazen Flight Lieutenant, still popular within the armed forces, ousted him, and took charge again. The first few years of his second administration were fraught with missteps such as setting up workers councils, and defense committees to monitor factory production and agricultural performance. The government had also levied price controls and subsidies in efforts to put a check on inflation. But, when it dawned on him that these populist measures weren't helping to lift the economy, Rawlings accepted the bitter pill of the IMF and World Bank, dropped the subsidies and price controls, and by the early 1990's, Ghana's economy was growing at one of the fastest rates on the African continent.

In 1992, Jerry Rawlings shed off his military fatigues, and was elected into office as a civilian president. He was re-elected for another 5-year term in 1996. By the time he relinquished office in 2001, Ghana's political landscape had changed significantly, allowing for smooth democratic transition from one leader to another. Successive leaders after Rawlings including, John Kufour, John Atta Mills, John Mahama, and the current one, Nana Akufo-Addo, have all been democratically elected under rules of universal suffrage. This is an exemplary feature that's a rarity on the African continent. The stability has also allowed the country's economy to perform above the sub-Saharan average growth rate. The World Bank estimated Ghana's Gross Domestic Product

(GDP) at US$ 47.3 billion, or a GDP per capita of $1,642 in 2017, with an annual growth rate of 8.5%. The economy has a rich agricultural and mineral base that has been tapped to provide diversification. In 2005, Ghana's economic fortunes improved even more when the nation struck offshore commercial quantities of crude oil.

Ghana's external debt stood at $23.1 billion, in 2017 or about 49% of GDP. The level of debt has accelerated fast, despite the country having been a beneficiary of massive write-offs from multi-lateral institutions such as the World Bank, IMF, and the Paris Club a decade ago. The main reason for this may be attributed to the continent-wide orientation towards China, which has allowed most low-income countries to obtain soft loans on terms less stringent than western institutions.

CHAPTER 10

Guinea was the second sub-Saharan African country to gain independence after Ghana, but the first of the Francophone west African countries to do so. French Guinea, or Guinea-Conakry, as it's often referred to, to distinguish it from Guinea-Bissau, gained its independence, fully divorcing itself from France on October 2, 1958, with Ahmed Sekou Touré as president. Fiercely nationalistic, he adapted the mantra:

"Poverty in liberty is better than wealth in slavery".

In his quest for total independence, Sekou Touré had rejected French President Charles de Gaulle's invitation to remain within the French Community even after gaining independence. For this, France retaliated by withdrawing not only economic aid to the newly independent nation, but also stripping and taking away anything movable that was associated with France, including, (it's alleged), light bulbs and electric sockets. The country's name was also changed from French Guinea to the Republic of Guinea to seal the divorce. Abandoned by the French, Sekou Touré forged a close friendship with Kwame Nkrumah who had secured his own country's independence only a year earlier. The two became strong advocates for African liberation and Pan-Africanism. Sekou Touré would later reciprocate the friendship when he hosted Nkrumah in exile after his ouster from power in 1966.

Sekou Touré's career started in the Trade Union movement in the 1940's, during which he successfully organized a labor strike in French West Africa against mainly French companies. Following a French policy initiated in the 1940's, some politicians in French colonies could serve in the French parliament. His first bitter encounter with the French happened in 1951, after he was denied taking a seat he had won in the national assembly in Paris. Re-elected to the same seat in 1954, but still prevented from occupying it, he was finally allowed to take his seat in 1956, following le Loi Cadre (legal reform) passed by the French National Assembly, a turning point between France and its foreign territorial possessions. By this time his blood was boiling over his mistreatment, and therefore, Sekou Touré was in no mood to accede to remaining within the French Community.

Under le Loi Cadre, France would continue controlling foreign affairs and currency in its foreign territories, which relegated them to a status of "junior partners" to France, something unacceptable to nationalistic Sekou Touré. The "Non" vote referendum was engineered by the Guinean branch of the Rassemblement Democratique Africain (RDA), which united French territories in west and central Africa. The Guinean branch was more radical under the stewardship of Sekou Touré.

But his anger was not limited to France only. As an abashed nationalist and anti-colonialist, he excoriated the United States for its alliances with western European colonial powers, and its continual dealings with South Africa, which had recently introduced the abhorrent policy of apartheid. Devoid of friends in the western-world and faced with a crumbling economy after France withdrew economic aid, Sekou Toure turned to the eastern bloc, especially the Soviet Union, although he had some flirtations with Mao Zedong's China as well. In the early 1960's, around half of Guinea's exports were purchased by eastern bloc countries. But even here, he didn't want to replace one colonial master with another, so he attempted to obtain aid by remaining non-aligned, sometimes playing one super-power against another. For instance, during the Cuban missile crisis, Sekou Touré refused to allow the Russians using Guinean airports as refueling stations on their way to Cuba.

Sekou Touré increasingly led Guinea with an iron fist, encircled by family and close associates. Growing opposition was mercilessly squashed, sometimes with executions. This became a common feature especially after 1971, when opposition dissidents based in neighboring Guinea Bissau, invaded Guinea in an attempt to topple the president. His regime soldiered on relentlessly under increasing opposition until his death in 1984. The Democratic Party of Guinea (PDG), by now severely weakened, could not survive the onslaught of opposition, and was toppled by a military coup barely one week after Sekou Touré's death. Colonel Lansana Conte took over and governed through a Military Committee for National Recovery. Conte embarked on transitioning the economy from the once rigidly state-controlled version to allowing private ownership and encouragement of international foreign direct investment (FDI). To boost his democratic credentials, he lifted the ban on opposition parties, allowing them to participate in an election, although he continued to control all state apparatus. A presidential election was conducted in 1993, which Conte won under his Party of Unity and Progress (PUP), using the power of incumbency, that left opposition parties disgruntled with claims of widespread electoral fraud.

His power was later challenged in 1996, this time, by the military whom he had denied a pay raise. Conte hid in an underground bunker for days after the military took over most installations in the capital, Conakry, and shelled the presidential palace. He was rescued by more loyal troops from upcountry, after conceding to their demands for higher pay. But his regime continued to be plagued by instability, interspersed with military attempts at coup d'états. President Conte died in office in 2008. His death was followed by yet another coup led by Moussa Dadis Camara, who in turn was injured in a counter-coup by his deputy, Sekouba Conate, who lasted until the presidential election held in December 2010.

Following that election, Alpha Conde, a long-time opposition leader who contested and lost twice against Lansana Conte in 1993 and 1998 took power. First elected in December 2010, he was re-elected to a second term in 2015.

Guinea continues to struggle under political instability. The West African nation has endured two military coup d'états in the last three years since the overthrow of Alpha Conde. Mamady Doumbouya, who took over as interim president on October 1, 2021, was removed by another military junta in September 2022.

Guinea's population is estimated at around 13.3 million, nearly 48% of whom live below the UN prescribed poverty line. The nation has a predominantly young population with a median age of 18.5 years, and growing at approximately 3.5 percent, one of the highest in the world. The economy has continued to under-perform, despite being endowed with vast amounts of mineral resources. The country is estimated to hold one quarter of the world's proven reserves of bauxite (the main ingredient in the production of aluminum). It also contains close to 2 billion tons of iron ore, diamond and uranium deposits. Part of this subpar performance may be attributed to the rampant civil wars that spilled over from neighboring Liberia and Sierra Leone beginning in the 1990's, plus the devastation emanating from the Ebola epidemic that lasted nearly two years, beginning from 2013, and lasting through 2016.

In the latest economic report from the African Development Bank, (2018), real GDP grew at an estimated rate of 5.9%. The main contribution to overall growth came from the industrial sector, which grew at 8.7%. The primary sector grew by 3.1%, while the services sector rose by 5.1%. The budget deficit doubled between 2017 and 2018, from 2.2% of GDP, to 4.4%, due to new loans to finance public investment, mainly infrastructure. This trend has been noticeable in a lot of African countries, hurriedly obtaining Chinese loans to boost infrastructure.

The country's debt burden stood at 39% of GDP, a 2% rise from the previous year. But this is still considered a moderate debt distress level. Inflation was kept in check by a restrictive monetary policy. Intra-regional exports to the Economic Community of West African States (ECOWAS) were a paltry 1%, the bulk of exports (96%) consisting of mineral products being sent to Asia, mainly China.

Despite the huge mining potential, with the mining sector accounting for 90% of Guinea's exports, it only generates 17% of the tax revenue, 12% of GDP, and only 2.6% of employment. A plan is underway to link electric grids within 7 countries, with Guinea at the center, exporting most of the power. However, infrastructural problems such as road links are still limiting the process.

CHAPTER 11

The Republic of Cameroon was the second Francophone West African country to gain independence after Guinea. That day came on January 1, 1960, when Ahmadou Ahidjo's party, Union Camerounaise steered the country to independence, although, unlike Guinea, it retained close links with France and the larger French Community.

The name Cameroon (Cameroun-French) was derived from the 15th century Portuguese explorer Fernando Po, who named the River Wouri, Rios dos Camaroes or shrimp river, due to the prevalence of many types of shrimp in this river.

The country had been penetrated by British and American missionaries in the early 19th century, but it was the Germans who became the first European power to colonize it and make commercial exploitation of its vast natural resources. They set up a warehouse near the mouth of the Wouri River, and as their numbers began to swell, they requested Chancellor Bismarck to set up a consul. Following the Berlin Conference of 1884, during which the scramble for Africa began in earnest, Bismarck decided to establish an African empire in competition with other European colonial powers.

Bismarck dispatched Gustav Nachtigal to Cameroon, to negotiate a treaty with some local chiefs, which would allow German acquisition of territory, and allow operations to take place smoothly. The next year, in 1885, the Chancellor sent a governor. However, all had not been smooth, as rivalry broke out with the chiefs that were not co-opted. They invaded the villages of those affiliated with the colonialists, and even brought down the German Flag, murdering the head of the German company, Woermann in the process. Angered by this, the Germans, whose ship, the Bismarck was off the coast, descended on the riotous chiefs in a feat of reprisals, setting villages ablaze, killing and brutalizing the local people.

Meantime, Germany also continued negotiations with both Britain and France regarding land bordering Cameroon. Ten years after the Berlin conference, the borders of Cameroon were drawn, including land ceded by the British from eastern Nigeria, and an even larger area covering 105,000 square miles, ceded by France from their Central African holdings. But the Germans left Cameroon mainly in the hands of commercial companies, whose sole motive was to maximize profits at the least cost, just like King Leopold of Belgium was doing in the Congo. Those companies granted concessions, set up large banana, rubber and cocoa plantations using forced labor on which many violations of human rights were rampant.

But Germany's fortunes were torpedoed when the 1st World War broke out in 1914. Britain and France, now allied against Germany, could not allow the latter to operate in its territories such as Togo and Cameroon, sandwiched between their own. In the 1919 Treaty of Versailles, Germany was stripped of all its African territorial possessions. Their administration was assigned to the League of Nations. Soon, however, the territories were apportioned between the British and French, since they were already adjacent to their own. Until independence in 1960, the British retained the administration of two thin strips of land east of the Benue River, that would later remain a source of headache to the leadership in Cameroon.

When the Union des Populations du Cameroun (UPC) agitated for independence beginning in 1958, the question remained as to what would happen in British-Administered western Cameroon. France granted independence to its own territory in 1960, and, one year later, in a plebiscite, the northern strip voted to join Nigeria, while the southern joined Cameroon to create The Federal Republic of Cameroon. President Ahidjo ruled for 22 years under this smoking cauldron, which he then passed on to Paul Biya in 1982.

Ahmadou Babatoura Ahidjo was born to a Fulani chief on August 24, 1924, in Garoua, a small inland river port on the Benue River in northern Cameroon. He attended secondary school in Yaonde with the intention of securing a mid-level job in the civil service. But when he failed to complete his education, he took on a job as a radio operator for the post office, staying on until 1946, when he decided to enter elective politics. In 1947, Ahidjo was elected to the then Trust territory's first Assembly and re-elected to the same position in 1952. He was subsequently elected to the Assembly of the French Union, where he first served as Secretary in 1954, and later elevated to vice-president for the 1956-57 session.

When Cameroon was granted self-government status in 1957, Andre Marie Mbida, leader of the Democrates Camerounais party assumed the premiership, with Ahidjo as his deputy. And, when Mbida was forced to resign in February 1958, Ahidjo took up the premiership. By then, he had formed his own party, Union Camerounais, which became the governing party when he replaced Mbida. On January 1, 1960, the former French Trust territory of Cameroon became an independent republic, and later that May, Ahidjo was elected as the first president. He went on to serve as the president of the Federal Republic, after the French Trust territory merged with the British Trust territory on October 1, 1961, a post he would retain until 1982.

Unlike current President Paul Biya's excesses, Ahidjo was not into flamboyancy and public ostentation, a quality that brought a sense of authority and dignity to his style. And, like Nkrumah and Sekou Touré, he espoused the philosophy of a one-party state, and the spirit of Pan-Africanism and African socialism. He used his stature to attempt a reconciliation between the minority Anglophone and the dominant Francophone regions. Above all, he voluntarily handed power to his successor, Paul Biya in 1982, although he stayed on as leader of the country's single party. A power struggle soon ensued, in which Ahidjo was accused of plotting to overthrow the government. Taking asylum in France in 1983, the Biya government sentenced him to death in absentia in 1984, but later commuted this to an indefinite life sentence. He never returned to Cameroon after that. He died of a heart attack in Dakar, Senegal, on November 30, 1989.

Under Biya, the English-speaking northwest and southwest regions were virtually ignored developmentally, their people sidelined, and any uprising seriously squashed. Sentiments by these Anglophone regions to secede have intensified during Biya's presidency, especially since 2017.Meanwhile, the octogenarian president has earned himself the moniker of "visiting president", due to his regular prolonged absence from, and short stopovers in Cameroon, spending more time in France than Cameroon. The northwestern region has been prone to attacks by the Boko Haram extremist group which operates in northeastern Nigeria and surrounding areas. The country has also clashed with Nigeria over the oil rich Bakassi peninsular whose territorial integrity both countries claim.

With 37 years of rule under his belt, Paul Biya ranks among the longest continuous ruling leaders on the continent, and the world. He has earned this longevity mainly through manipulation of the electoral process. He has also taken advantage of the internal divisions between the Francophone and Anglophone communities, remnants of the colonial period's divide and rule policies. His party, Cameroon People's Democratic Movement (CPDM), plays a dominant role in the country, controlling 148 out the 180 seats in the National Assembly, and 81 out of 100 in the Senate.

The nation of 24 million is endowed with natural resources including oil, gas, other minerals, and high value supplies of timber. Oil constitutes about 40% of exports, which has caused the total value of exports to suffer, since the price of oil plummeted in 2014. Real GDP registered a growth of only 3.8% in 2018, although this was an improvement over the prevailing period where growth was flat. The uptick was attributed to a new offshore liquified natural gas (LNG) field coming on board, and increased demand of agricultural products by neighbors, including Nigeria, Chad and Central African Republic. On the downside, the country's poverty-reduction rate fell short of the population growth rate, causing poverty to increase by 12% to about 8.1 million (30%) of the population between 2007 and 2014.This poverty is concentrated in the northern regions, where 56% of the population is rated poor. Economic prospects won't improve much, perhaps until President Biya leaves office, and the underlying problems of the insurgency are internally resolved.

CHAPTER 12

If Cote d'Ivoire was the crowning jewel of Francophone west Africa, Abidjan its capital was le grand ville de Savannah. In pre-colonial times, the country flourished as the Kingdom of Gyaaman, with its capital Bondoukou serving as a center for trade and Islamic scholarship. These developments were disrupted during the 19th century, as European powers scrambled to cut up and divide pieces of the so-called Dark Continent amongst themselves. French colonial rule was established over the country in 1893. For the period between 1904-1958, Cote d'Ivoire was rolled into the Federation of Francophone West Africa. The citizens of these countries were exposed to the French policy of assimilation. The French language and culture were prioritized over the subjects, but without fully extending the rights of citizenship.

By the end of the second world war, Ivorians were recognized as French citizens, and granted the right to organize themselves politically. Inspired by events in neighboring Ghana, and Guinea, both of which had recently gained independence, Cote d'Ivoire, too was agitating for autonomy, and was finally granted full independence on August 7, 1960, with Felix Houphouet-Boigny as president.

Felix Houphouet-Boigny, affectionately referred to as "Le Vieux Grand Homme" (The Great Old Man), or Papa, was born in Yamoussoukro on October 18, 1905, the son of a Baoule tribal chief. He organized the first Trade Union in 1944, and was, thereafter, elected to the French Parliament, and subsequently appointed a minister in the French Government, the first African to serve in a European cabinet. In 1946, he was one of the founders of Rassemblement Democratique Africain or African Democratic Rally (RDA) a West African umbrella group that sought to fight for equal rights for Africans. In Cote d'Ivoire, he formed a local chapter known as Parti Democratique de Cote d'Ivoire (PDCI) with the same objectives and aspirations.

Upon taking the reins of power at independence on August 7, 1960, Houphouet-Boigny governed skillfully, balancing the delicate forces between ethnic and religious sectors that have torn many countries apart. He used those skills to reconcile with domestic opponents, as well as settling disputes among neighbors. Aided by goodwill from France, and favorable prices of the country's main exports of cocoa and coffee, he steered the country towards prosperity. This helped stabilize conditions at home, allowing him the mandate to serve many terms during his tenure in office. Nonetheless, during the latter part of the 1980's, his dominant ruling party, le PDCI, began to run into the headwinds of multi-party democracy that were sweeping across the continent. In 1990, Houphouet-Boigny defeated Professor Laurent Gbagbo of the Ivorian Popular Front (FPI) in the first multi-party election. The election was challenged in court and affirmed in favor of the incumbent. However, it left Le Vieux with a scar that has come to characterize the invincible "Big man" of African politics, where the incumbent never loses an election because he controls all the state apparatus.

Although Houphouet-Boigny is credited with putting the Ivorian economy on a sound footing during his 33-year rule, he was criticized for missteps such as building a grand monument to himself in a small city such as his birthplace, Yamoussoukro. Le Basillique Notre-Dame de la Paix (Basilica of Our Lady of Peace) true cost is unknown but is variously estimated to be somewhere between $200-$600 million. Modeled on Saint Peter's Basilica at the Vatican, the 320,000 square foot edifice was built between 1985-89, and was consecrated in 1990 by Pope John Paul II. Out of the country's 24 million people, the catholic population constitutes about 52%, with 25% belonging to the Islamic faith, and the remaining not fitting the two major categories.

The president died in office in 1993, half-way through his 7th term. He was replaced by Henri Konan Bedie, president of the National Assembly, and, like the president himself, belonged to the PDCI party, and a fellow Baoule. In 1995, the country went through a controversial election boycotted by the main opposition parties. The boycott revolved around the government's attempt to re-write the constitution to exclude certain groups and individuals such as current President Alassane Ouattara from participating. Konan Bedie won the race, but ethnic tensions continued boiling. Then, on December 23, 1999, with tensions at near breaking point, a military mutiny was led by Brig-General Robert Guei, who seized power from Konan Bedie,

General Guei who had pledged to hand-over power to an elected civilian in the 2000 election, changed his mind, participated in the election, and lost to Professor Laurent Gbagbo. Two years later, General Guei engineered a coup attempt against President Gbagbo, in which the General lost his life. Although Gbagbo's presidency was saved, the coup set a stage for the civil war that ensued afterwards. The country was split in two along ethnic divisions, with rebels holding the north, while government forces controlled the south. Peacekeepers drawn from both France and the Economic Community for West Africa (ECOWAS), were brought in to maintain peace along a buffer zone the UN designated as a "zone of confidence".

However, a truce between the two antagonists negotiated in 2003 soon fell apart, mainly over the government's intransigence over who qualified to run for the presidency in a national election. Tensions further escalated after the government bombed rebel-held positions in the north in 2004. Matters worsened when an accidental bombing of French gendarmes by the government, caused France to retaliate. Anti-French sentiments rose, followed by riots against French interests in the country. Another peace agreement negotiated in South Africa in 2005 could not be implemented fast enough, leading to an extension of President Gbagbo's term to 2007. When talks resumed in Burkina Faso, a power-sharing arrangement was struck, in which Gbagbo would retain the presidency, while Guillaume Soro, the rebel leader became Prime Minister. The new government was meant to be temporary until elections were held ten months later. But the sluggish pace of voter registration, compounded by issues of legitimacy of who qualified to run for the top job further delayed elections until October 31, 2010.

The election pitted three headstrong men with a reserve of antagonism against one another, paving the way for a messy outcome. Neither of the main contenders, Gbagbo, Ouattara or Bedie scored enough votes in the first round to give him a mandate to govern, so a runoff was scheduled for November 28, 2010, between Gbagbo and Ouattara, the two top scorers. But Gbagbo, perhaps sensing defeat, challenged the yet announced results, claiming there was a lot of fraud and voter intimidation in the north, where Ouattara drew most support. Meanwhile, international observers certified the results in which Ouattara garnered 54% as fair and representing the will of the people. Nevertheless, using a series of legal maneuvers, such as an appeal through the Constitutional Council, which discarded a portion of the results, Gbagbo was declared the winner with 51%.

Gbagbo, using the power of incumbency and state apparatus, was sworn in for a third term. But Ouattara, who enjoyed both international and northern rebel support, also got sworn in as a parallel government. Calls were mounted on Gbagbo to step down, and when this failed, organizations such as ECOWAS and the African Union suspended Cote d'Ivoire's membership. Beyond that, travel bans were imposed on the government by western countries, as were financial squeezes from multi-lateral lenders such as the IMF (Ouattara's former employer), the World Bank, and the African Development Bank (AfDB). The stalemate began to take both a human and economic toll, as government soldiers committed gross human rights on the opposition, while the once vibrant economy went into a tailspin. In 2011, major international banks began closing their operations in the country. The AfDB, headquartered in the capital Abidjan, evacuated most of its staff and relocated them to Tunis, Tunisia. However, the coup de grace happened when Ouattara appealed to the international community to implement a boycott of Ivorian cocoa exports. Cote d'Ivoire is the leading world producer of cocoa beans.

But, despite all the hurdles placed in his path, Gbagbo was prepared to soldier on. Pro-Gbagbo forces continued escalating the violence by attacking any suspected pockets of Ouattara supporters, including those attending rallies, going as far as cutting off utility services areas dominated by his opponent's supporters. These actions were soon reciprocated by the rebels who took the fight to government soldiers, capturing government-held territory, one square mile at a time. By March 2011, the rebels, known as Forces Republicaines de Cote d'Ivoire (FRCI), had captured more than two thirds of the country, including the political capital of Yamoussoukro. The rebels then prepared for the battle to capture the commercial capital of Abidjan in the next few weeks. Their activities were aided by UN and French bombings of government strongholds such as military bases.

In his last-ditch effort to retain control, Gbagbo pushed government soldiers to attack Ouattara's base of operation which was protected by UN peacekeepers. This provoked response that included attacking Gbagbo's residence, resulting in the arrest of the president and his wife Simone. Ouattara was now in charge, and he would immediately embark on the process of healing a broken nation. Sanctions imposed on the country during Gbagbo's holdout were lifted, and the country was re-admitted to both ECOWAS and the African Union. In early May, the Constitutional Council which had sided with Gbagbo in the December election, finally reversed itself and recognized Ouattara as the legitimate president. He was inaugurated on May 21, 2011.

Gbagbo was taken into custody by the International Criminal Court (ICC) at The Hague in the Netherlands, where he languished for five years while awaiting trial. The joint trial with his associate, Charles Ble Goude, started in January 2016, but were both acquitted in January 2019. His wife, Simone, was tried in an Ivorian court in 2015, sentenced to 20 years in jail. She was later acquitted in 2017, the acquittal overturned, in July 2018, but later released along with 800 other Ivorians in an amnesty offered by President Ouattara in August 2018.

President Ouattara won another term in 2015 after his party entered a coalition with Houphouet-Boigny's PDCI. Then, in 2016, a new constitution was promulgated, among whose roles was to straighten out the contentious issue of who qualifies as an Ivorian citizen. The country has regained its position as the largest economy among the West African Economic and Monetary Union, a distant second to Nigeria, and the AfDB staff have resumed their operations at their headquarters in Abidjan.

According to the World Bank, Cote d'Ivoire's economic outlook for 2018 showed a dynamic picture with a growth rate of about 7.4%, the highest among the West African Economic and Monetary Union (WAEMU). This marked the seventh consecutive year that the economy delivered a growth rate above 7%. During this period, GDP per capita grew an astounding 32%. Current trends point towards the economy remaining healthy, provided external factors do not change drastically. An agrarian-based economy, the country ranks as the world's top producer of cocoa and cashew nuts. It is also among the top three coffee exporters on the African continent.

Despite this robust growth, however, the level of poverty remains high, having fallen from 51% to 46% between 2008 and 2015. To put it in context, this means around 10.7 million Ivorians live on less than $1.50 a day. The poverty figures also show high regional disparities, with the northern region at nearly 60%, while coastal and southwestern regions are close to 40%. The country is undergoing rapid urbanization, with the two largest cities of Abidjan and Yamoussoukro experiencing population explosions with their attending problems. Cote d'Ivoire only trails Cameroon and Ghana in urbanization on the continent.

The country's GDP was estimated at $43,1 billion dollars with a per capita income of around $1,632. This is expected to rise to $47 billion dollars by 2020. Public debt stood at around 46.4% of GDP, with the budget deficit running at an average 3.7% of GDP.

CHAPTER 13

Benjamin Nnamdi Azikiwe (popularly known as Zik), was a Nigerian statesman who began his career in newspapers before diving into politics. Born in the northern town of Zungeru, Niger State, on November 16,1904, he attended his early education in Onitsha and Calabar in Igboland before proceeding to Lagos for secondary school. In 1925, he traveled to the United States, enrolling at Lincoln University in Philadelphia, where he earned both a bachelor's and master's degree, and went on to earn another master's from the University of Pennsylvania. He returned to West Africa in 1934 and established a nationalistic newspaper in the Gold Coast (later renamed Ghana). He even became a mentor to the man who would later become Ghana's first president, Kwame Nkrumah. It is worth noting that Nkrumah also attended Lincoln University and U-Penn.

Azikiwe returned to his native Nigeria in 1937 and continued in the newspaper business for a while before joining the Nigeria Youth Movement, and then in 1944, became one of the founders of the National Council of Nigeria and the Cameroons (NCNC), along with luminary nationalist Herbert Macaulay. The party's objective under

Macaulay's stewardship, was clear. They needed to wrest power from the colonialists, who had used divisive machinations to subjugate, divide, and turn even the once peaceful ethnic groups against each other for the purpose of ruling the country. Upon Macaulay's death in 1946, Azikiwe took over the leadership of the party, but continued with the same zeal of obtaining independence for Nigeria.

That day came on October 1, 1960, when Britain finally granted independence to Nigeria. The 1959 elections had failed to yield a majority position for any of the two main competing parties, Azikiwe's NCNC, or Abubakar Tafawa Balewa's Northern People's Congress (NPC). What resulted was a coalition government, with Tafawa Balewa as Prime Minister, and Nnamdi Azikiwe holding the mainly ceremonial position of President of the Senate. In a June 1961 United Nations-supervised referendum over the status of northern Trust Territory of Cameroon, they chose to join the northern region of Nigeria, while in October, the southern part joined Cameroon. Nigeria became a Republic on October 1, 1963, and Azikiwe became the first president of the country, while Balewa retained the more powerful Premiership.

Following independence, there was a lull, but this honeymoon didn't last very long. A 1962-63 population census revealed many regional developmental disparities that sparked off some tribal tensions. An attempt to diffuse this tension was made by subdividing the western region into two which only turned out to be a band-aid approach. The figures exposed major regional educational and economic imbalances among the three main ethnic groups, namely the Yoruba of the west, the Igbo of the east, and the Hausa-Fulani of the northern region. The leaders of these ethnic groups were suspicious of each other and were adamant about controlling their turf. While for instance, the southerners complained of northern political domination, the Hausa-Fulani were suspicious of southern elites capturing power and denying them resources from oil for developing the north. The first oil discovery in Nigeria was made by Shell-BP Company in 1956, at Oloibiri in the Niger Delta.

By 1964, political chaos was unfolding in Yorubaland, resulting in a boycott of Federal elections in December that year. As order continued to deteriorate, a group of army officers led the first coup attempt against the Federal government during which Prime Minister Tafawa Balewa (a northerner), was assassinated, along with two other regional premiers. In January 1966, a group of mostly Igbo army officers led by Lt-Col Odumegwu Ojukwu, took over the federal government, but were forced to hand power to the more senior Major-Gen Johnson Aguiyi-Ironsi, a fellow Igbo. An attempt by Gen Ironsi to abolish federalism and rule under a unitary government was rebuffed. The army was also accused of favoring a government dominated by Igbos from the east. Only six months after the January coup, a combination of northern Hausa and western Yoruba officers, fearing Igbo domination, staged a countercoup, in which Gen Ironsi himself was assassinated. The head of the new military government was Gen Yakubu Gowon. Gen Ironsi had appointed Lt-Col Ojukwu as the military governor of the mostly Igbo eastern region, and even when Gowon took over, he left him in that position.

By now, tensions were searing so high, fueled by internecine violence in the north, and threats of secession by the Igbo in the east. That October, Gen Gowon called a conference to determine the constitutional future of the country, which disbanded after ethnic assassinations were conducted, mainly on Igbos. To neutralize the power of regions, General Gowon subdivided each of the existing four regions into three states, creating a total of twelve states under the Federal Republic umbrella. In January 1967, another conference was held at Aburi in Ghana to no effect, after Lt.-Col Ojukwu leading the Eastern delegation (Igbos), couldn't agree on the accords. Five months after the Aburi meeting, on May 30, 1967, the Eastern region's Assembly (now three states) authorized Ojukwu to set up a new sovereign Republic of Biafra, ushering in what would be perhaps, the most devastating and protracted civil war in Nigerian history.

Fighting broke out in July, between the Federal army and the Biafran rebels, escalating into a full-fledged war after the rebels crossed the Niger River, temporarily seizing Benin City in Ondo State, before being pushed back. After this incident, the Federal army launched an offensive that captured Enugu, the designated capital of Biafra with a hope that the humiliating blow would end the rebellion, but it did not. The shelling of rebel strongholds, and the devastation of villages in the Igbo heartland seemed to harden the rebels' fighting spirit that resulted in a stalemate for the two and a half years of the rebellion. But there was widespread suffering and death from war atrocities, including disease and starvation visited on the victims of the war, on both sides.

For two years, mediation efforts by the Organization of African Unity (OAU) and such bodies as the UN had failed in their attempts to stop the war. However, in December 1969, the Federal army, sensing a severe shortage of food and ammunition on the rebel side, launched a major offensive that delivered the coup de grace to the Biafran rebels. By now, controlling only a small fraction of the original territory, and his people on the verge of starvation, Gen Ojukwu abandoned the effort on January 11, 1970, and fled into exile in Cote d'Ivoire. His deputy surrendered to the Federal government in Lagos on January 15, 1970.

Gen Gowon, now in full control of the country, made every effort to reconcile and heal a torn-apart nation without assigning blame to any side. Helped by booming oil prices from OPEC's oil embargo launched in 1973, the Federal government spared little effort in rebuilding some of the infrastructure destroyed during the war. He even postponed elections slated for 1974, and pushed the schedule to 1976, to allow more time for the nation to heal. However, in true Nigerian fashion, in July 1975, while Gowon was away, attending the Annual OAU Conference in Kampala, Uganda, he was overthrown by the military. (This author, then a student at Makerere University in Kampala, learned firsthand about the incident from a Nigerian Igbo classmate, who had just been to Apollo Hotel, now Sheraton, where Gowon was supposed to address Nigerian nationals in Uganda). From Kampala, Gen Gowon flew into exile in Britain, where he pursued a PhD program.

Chief Chukwuemeka Odumegwu Ojukwu, was born to a wealthy Igbo businessman in Zungeru, Nigeria, on November 4, 1933. He attended Oxford University in England, graduating in 1955, and returned to his homeland where he first served as an administrator. He joined the Nigerian Army in 1957 and was promoted quickly to senior officer ranks. From the fall of Biafra in 1970, until 1982 when he was pardoned, he lived in exile in Cote d'Ivoire. After the pardon, he returned to Nigeria, and attempted several times to enter elective office without success. He died in a London hospital on November 26, 2011, at the age of 78.

Some of the dreadful atrocities of the Nigeria-Biafran civil war are well-dramatized in Chimamanda Ngozi Adichie's best-selling book, titled, "Half of A Yellow Sun". Adichie is an Igbo born in Enugu City, once the capital of Biafra.

Following Gowon's ouster, the Army installed Brig-Gen Murtala Ramat Muhammed as the new head of state. He is credited with starting the process of moving the Federal capital to Abuja, leaving congested Lagos as the Commercial center. He also initiated a process of returning government to civilian rule, but was assassinated in February 1976, in a failed coup attempt. The army continued to rule under Lt-Gen Olusegun Obasanjo, who continued the transfer path left by his predecessor.

Born on March 5, 1937, in Abeokuta, Ogun State, Obasanjo attended local schools, including Baptist Boys High School before joining the Nigerian Army in 1958. While in the army, he was sent to attend top British Military Colleges, including the Royal College of Military Engineers at Chatham, and the Royal College of Defense Studies, London. He grew through the ranks, and had an illustrious career, including serving as part of a contingent of United Nations officers seconded to the Congo (now Democratic Republic of Congo), during turbulences that followed the assassination of Patrice Lumumba, its first Prime Minister. Between 1969-70, Obasanjo served as the Commander, Third Commando Marine Division, Southeastern State during the Nigerian civil war with breakaway Biafra. It was Gen Obasanjo, who accepted the surrender of Biafran officers on January 12, 1970.

Under Obasanjo's leadership, the British Parliamentary style of choosing the country's leader was replaced with an American style of direct Presidential elections. The political space was opened so that many parties would compete in the presidential elections to return the country to civilian rule. Among the five which were finally selected and registered were, the National Party of Nigeria (NPN), headed by Alhaji Shehu Shagari. During the 1979 election, Shagari's party edged out Chief Obafemi Awolowo's United Party of Nigeria (UPN), catapulting Shagari into the presidency. Gen Obasanjo who had failed to win the presidency on a civilian ticket, dutifully handed over the reins of power to Shehu Shagari. The world was in a recession, and the oil boom Nigeria had enjoyed during most of the 1970's, was beginning to fizzle. Nonetheless, Shagari and his cronies used their access to state resources to line up their pockets in a manner that even overwhelmed scandal-laden Nigeria. One official described Shagari's administration like this:

"While previous regimes stole with a spoon, Shagari's used a shovel".

Shagari managed to maneuver his way through re-election in1983, but the souring economic environment, coupled with hysteria against a looting and unscrupulous regime, created conditions for yet another chance for military intervention. On December 31, 1983, a young Major-General named Muhammadu Buhari, staged a coup that removed the Shagari regime, citing looting the treasury and incessant corruption as the main reason for the army's action. The General would later transform himself into a civilian and run again on his anti-corruption manifesto. At the time of writing this, (September 16, 2019), Alhaji Buhari is enjoying his second term as a popularly elected president of Nigeria. His term as a military head of state lasted from December 31, 1983, to August 27, 1985. He was toppled in a military coup.

Maj-Gen Buhari was followed by another military General called Ibrahim Badamasi Babangida, who stayed on from August 27, 1985, to August 26, 1993. He was Chief of Staff of the Army prior to taking office under pressure for the country to return to civilian rule. To prepare the country for an election, Babangida appointed a well-respected lawyer and businessman named Ernest Adegunle Shonekan as interim president, who lasted only three months on the job, from August 26, 1993, to November 17, 1993, as yet another military strongman sought to place himself at the helm.

Of all the military leaders that have ruled Nigeria since independence, no name brings more chills to Nigerians and the broader international community than that of Gen Sani Abacha. Born on September 20, 1943, in Kano State, Abacha received his military training from both

Nigerian and British military institutions. In 1983, then at the rank of Brigadier, he collaborated with Gen. Babangida in overthrowing the civilian government of Shehu Shagari and installing Gen. Buhari. Two years later, he again collaborated with Gen. Babangida in removing Buhari, only this time around, Babangida installed himself, with Abacha as his second-in-command. Babangida was increasingly under pressure to return the country to civilian rule. However, when the election conducted in August 1993 was won by business tycoon Moshood Abiola, Babangida and Abacha denied him the keys to Aso Rock (granite rock that features prominently behind presidential palace in Abuja). Instead, Babangida appointed another prominent lawyer and business statesman called Ernest Adegunle Shonekan to run the government on an interim basis. Elections in Nigeria, as elsewhere in Africa, are always haunted with a tribal element.

But Abacha kept his eyes on the prize, and three months later, he pushed Shonekan out, installed himself as president, and threw Chief Abiola and other prominent contestants in the most recent election, such as Gen. Olusegun Obasanjo into jail, charging them with treason. Nobel Laureate Wole Soyinka escaped jail by slipping out of the country, just in time. Both Abiola and Obasanjo hailed from Abeokuta, Ogun State, and once edited their high school newspaper, the Trumpeter together at the Baptist Boys High School. Chief Abiola, a Glasgow University-trained chartered accountant met his mysterious death in prison on July 7,1998, the day he was set to be released. Abacha himself had died under suspicious circumstances in the presidential palace on June 8, 1998, (some sources say, died in the presence of ladies of ill repute). Apart from heading one of the most corrupt regimes, (over $700 million in cash was recovered from State House following his death), Abacha became notorious for the hanging of prominent Ogoni environmentalist activist Ken Saro-Wiwa for opposing government and Shell Oil's pollution in the Ogoni region and the Niger delta, despite appeals from luminary figures including Pope John-Paul II and Mother Teresa.

General Abdulsalam Abubakar who succeeded Sani Abacha on June 8, 1998, accelerated the return to civilian rule by organizing an election in May 1999, which saw Gen Olusegun Obasanjo return to power as an elected civilian leader under the People's Democratic Party (PDP). Obasanjo ruled for two full terms, becoming the first elected president to do so since Nigeria's independence. This once again instilled confidence in the nation's governance, ushering in a semblance of stability that has allowed the nation to change its leadership in a peaceful and democratic manner. Obasanjo, (nicknamed Baba Africa), was in power from May 29, 1999, to May 29, 2007, when he peacefully handed over power to Umaru Musa Yar'Adua.

Umaru Yar'Adua was previously Governor of the northern state of Katsina and was installed as president on May 29, 2007, on a PDP ticket. Barely a year and a half into his term, the president flew to Saudi Arabia to seek treatment for previously undisclosed health problems and ended up staying for a year. On February 24, 2010, with pressure mounting for him to either return and run the country or step down, his plane touched down at Abuja International Airport in the dead of the night to shield the gravely ill president from the gaze of the curious public. The president never regained his strength. He died in Aso Presidential Palace on May 5, 2010.

Vice President Goodluck Azikiwe Jonathan who had been running the country during Yar'Adua's long hospitalization period, was elevated to President, and continued serving until he contested and lost against Muhammadu Buhari in 2015. President Buhari, who has subjected his compatriots to many health-related stays of his own in London, was recently re-elected to his second term as a civilian leader, and was sworn in on May 29, 2019, despite his failure to defeat the extremist group Boko Haram. The abduction of 276 girls from Chibok High School, a secondary school in north-eastern Nigeria by this group on April 14, 2014, caused a worldwide uproar, that involved no less a celebrity than US First Lady Michelle Obama donning a T-shirt emblazoned with the hash tag "Bring Back Our Girls". Buhari's popularity derives from the no-nonsense approach to Nigeria's incurable corruption, which image he cultivated when he first served as a military head of state back in the 1980's. But as of this writing, a citizens' case is being launched in the High Court against the country's legislators for their planned scheme to purchase luxury cars fully paid by taxpayers, despite biting poverty.

Nigeria ranks as Africa's largest economy, and, at nearly 200 million people, it also has the continent's largest population. To put it in context, its economy represents about 20% of the continental economic size, and 75% of the ECOWAS block. The country's oil-dependent economy continues to tag its fortunes on oil prices. Nigeria is a member of OPEC, and is the continent's largest oil exporter, (average 2 million b/day) on top of having the largest reserves of proven natural gas (5,111 bcm). The oil sector continues to be riddled with corruption that undercuts its potential to generate sustained high revenues, due to, among other ills, large thefts of crude oil. Earlier this month, (October 2022), authorities at the Nigerian Oil Corporation announced the discovery of an underwater 4-kilometer oil pipeline the shipping terminal, suspected to have existed for nearly a decade, and siphoning off thousands of barrels of oil per day. Nigeria's position as the continent's largest oil producer was recently overtaken by Angola. The sector continues to suffer due to low infrastructure investment.

The African Development Bank (AfDB) projects real GDP to grow at 2.3% in 2019, followed by a 2.4% growth in 2020. The IMF estimates 2.1% and 2.5% for 2019 and 2020, respectively. The country's GDP managed to grow by a rate 3.6% in 2021, buoyed by a 4.4% growth in the non-oil sector. The oil sector contracted by 8.3%. The performance is subpar for an economy playing catchup on many levels. Among the government's priorities, is creating steady employment for one of the world's youngest populations, driven by a population growing at around 2.6% p.a. President Buhari's latest re-election manifesto continues the vow of diversifying the economy away from the near stranglehold of oil dependency, an issue that has remained elusive to those before him. There are no clear indications of strategies to achieve this goal. The nation's public debt burden of around $73 billion (17.5% of GDP), is considered manageable, but it is growing due to the pent-up demand to modernize infrastructure. Also, persistent attacks by the Boko Haram extremist group on government institutions and other sections of the population in the northeast, create economic disruptions and the need for supplementary budgets. The need for continual military presence has raised defense expenditures in the national budget. This takes away resources that would be channeled into priority areas such as health, education, and environmental protection. The country's industrial production continues to be hamstrung by low power supplies, despite the nation's endowment with energy resources. Internet penetration stood at nearly 92.3 million people (47%) of the population in 2018 and growing fast. This is the largest volume in any single country on the continent. However, further access may remain limited by the legendary blackouts caused by the intermittent supply of electric power.

CHAPTER 14

For the longest period since its independence in 1960, the name Congo/Zaire, and now renamed Democratic Republic of Congo, (DRC), has been associated with poor governance, disorder, and chaos. The nation gained its independence from Belgium on June 30, 1960, with Joseph Kasavubu as President, and Patrice Lumumba as Prime Minister. But the honeymoon was practically over before it began, as the zeitgeist forces of the cold war unfolded, plunging the country at the center of the proxy wars between the two super-powers, namely the United States and the Soviet Union. The last year of the Eisenhower Administration had hoped to see this vast country of immense natural resources install a pro-western leadership at independence. However, many of the new African leaders agitating for independence, frustrated with western colonialism, were willing to flirt with the communism and socialism ideologies from the Soviet Union and China. Meanwhile, the Americans were determined to create a buffer which would serve as a bastion of opposition against this new encroaching force on the African continent.

On July 5, 1960, barely a week into independence, Congolese soldiers of the Force Publique mutinied against their Belgian commanders at the Thysville military base, demanding higher pay and better conditions. This sparked off insurrections on other bases throughout the country, and a sessional declaration of independence by the mineral-rich provinces of Katanga and Kasai. The saga quickly degenerated into anti-Belgian, anti-white violence, causing a stampede and an exodus among the white (mostly Belgian community). Belgium sought to restore order by rushing in troops, without consulting either President Kasavubu or Prime Minister Patrice Lumumba. To counter the Belgian invasion, the Lumumba government appealed for help from the United Nations. A resolution known as Organisations des Nations Unities au Congo (ONUC) was tabled on July 13 to establish an intervention force, and asked Belgium to withdraw its troops.

Lumumba's affiliations with the Soviet Union were already well-documented before he took over as prime minister. He had invited hordes of Soviet technicians and advisors into the country, which had alarmed western diplomats. So, when the mutinies started, the CIA station master alerted Washington that a full-scale Soviet invasion was imminent and needed to be stopped. The Prime Minister was invited to Washington to attempt winning him over towards western ideology. Meanwhile, ground preparations by the CIA and its internal collaborators were underway to remove Lumumba by any means, including an assassination, if warranted. Kasavubu initiated the move by dismissing Lumumba from the premiership on September 5, 1960, but Lumumba ignored the action and instead, reciprocated by trying to expel the president.

These actions prompted Col Joseph Desire Mobutu, to mount a military coup in collaboration with the CIA, purportedly to avert a civil war. Mobutu immediately expelled the Soviets, and upon an allegation of an assassination plot by Lumumba and his supporters against Mobutu, Lumumba was arrested, tortured, and ultimately brutally killed on January 17, 1961. The Republic of Congo was thrown into utter chaos after Lumumba's murder. Mr. Dag Hjalmar Hammarskjold, a Swedish national, who was serving his second term as the second United Nations Secretary General, was killed in a plane crash in Ndola, Zambia, on

September 18, 1961, while on his way to cease-fire negotiations. The Congo crisis had drawn in foreign fighters and mercenaries on both sides of the political divide, according to a book written by Bob Astles a British citizen who lived in Uganda during that period. He was close to the late President Milton Obote, and later acted as President Idi Amin's de facto Chief of Staff and trusted advisor after Amin staged a military coup of his own in January 1971 that toppled President Milton Obote. Bob was in position to know the goings-on because his wife, Mary Senkatuka Astles, served in Amin's cabinet.

Any attempts by the US and former colonial power Belgium, to stabilize the country with pro-western prime ministers such as Moise Kapenda Tshombe failed to deliver stability. However, fearing the rapid spread of communism on the African continent, the US and its European allies, (primarily Belgium in this case), set out to prop men like Mobutu as bastions of anti-communism. His position as a military strongman was further enhanced through a US-Congolese bilateral military agreement with the Kennedy Administration. Tired of bickering between President Kasavubu and Prime Minister Tshombe, Mobutu staged a second coup d'état on November 24, 1965, in which he dismissed both officials, and installed himself as the country's President with executive powers.

But, unlike Lumumba, Tshombe had survived the coup and fled to Spain, from where he continued to exert influence over the political direction of the newly independent country. In July 1966, 2,000 of Tshombe's Katanga gendarmes, aided by mercenaries, staged a mutiny in Kisangani. Although Mobutu's army crushed the rebellion, it would be followed by another one, again in Kisangani a year later. This second uprising was triggered by a rumor that alleged that Tshombe's plane, while on its way back to Congo, was hijacked over the Mediterranean, diverted to Algiers, where Tshombe died of a heart attack. The leader of this mutiny was a Belgian settler named Jean Schramme. About 100 former Katangese gendarmes, plus 1,000 other mutineers, held sway against Mobutu's nearly 32,000 troops of Armee Nationale Congolaise (ANC). This lasted until November 1967, when they crossed into neighboring Rwanda, and surrendered themselves to the authorities there. But Schramme escaped, and later turned up in Brazil, where the Belgian government spent years in fruitless attempts to extradite him back to Congo for trial.

For the next several years, until 1971, there was a lull, and a semblance of stability that allowed President Mobutu to consolidate his power. In 1971, he declared his "authenticity" policy, in which he changed the country's name to Zaire, and his own name to Mobutu Sese Seko Kuku Ngbendu wa za Banga, literally translating into "the cock that leaves no hen untouched". Mobutu's sole single party, la Mouvement Populaire de la Revolution (MPR) which remained in place until 1990, was characterized by corruption and patronage, with Mobutu himself as a cult symbol, donning his uniquely tailored African attire, topped by a leopard skin cap, and holding a curved walking stick under his left armpit, (captured very well in the comedy movie Coming to America, featuring James Earl Jones, Eddie Murphy, and Arsenio Hall). Mobutu spared no efforts to lavish himself and his entourage with luxuries, even when the rest of the country was wallowing in abject poverty. His Grand Chateau at his ancestral village of Gbadolite, for instance, was modeled on the palace at Versailles, and he was known to charter the French Concorde, to fly dignitaries there, to be entertained with culinary delights prepared by French chefs, washed down by champagne and caviar.

For instance, in 1975, while in Kampala to attend the annual conference of the Organization of African Unity (OAU), Mobutu's delegation rejected the 200-series Mercedes Benz car offered to other heads of state by Idi Amin (no less a showman), as the mode of transportation for their leader, calling it "unbefitting the status of their leader", and instead flew in a fleet of top of the line 500-series. The delegation also brought in two buses with bands that blasted their gyrating soukous music in the streets of Kampala, much to the relief of gazing crowds, including this author, who was then a young student attending Makerere University.

It's no secret that most African leaders (and other third world countries), take advantage of their positions to feather their nests from their countries' treasuries. In Africa, the few obvious exceptions to this rule have been Mwalimu Julius Nyerere of Tanzania, successive presidents of Botswana, and without a doubt, President Nelson Mandela of South Africa. But when it came to syphoning from the treasury, Mobutu seemed to occupy a special place of his own. His kleptocracy continued to thrive until the end of the cold war. During the time I worked at the World Bank in the 1980's, and 90's, a period sadly referred to as "the lost decade" for Africa, when most sub-Saharan countries including Congo-Zaire were teetering on bankruptcy, Mobutu was estimated to hold close to US$5 billion in Swiss and other offshore banks. At the same time, Congo was falling behind in servicing its external debts totaling less than that amount. In 1991, France reduced its funding to the country, and both the World Bank and IMF cut ties to the country, after Mobutu misappropriated $400 million from Gecamines, the state mining corporation. The joke at the time, was that only Mobutu could save his country by returning to the treasury, what he had taken out.

In 1977, the opposition movement party, known as Front de la Liberation Nationale Congolaise (FLNC), then exiled in Luanda, the Angolan capital, invaded the Katanga region, then known as Shaba province. Moroccan troops were flown in to restore stability in the area. But the following year, in May 1978, opposition rebels launched another invasion, once again in the Shaba province, occupying the town of Kolwezi for some time. Over 100 Europeans and hundreds of Congolese were taken hostage, and later slaughtered by the rebels and this time, Mobutu was able to suppress the rebellion with help from French gendarmes.

After 1991, his former supporters, primarily, the US, France and Belgium lost appetite for promoting strongmen. Some went as far as rendering support to Mobutu's rivals such as Etienne Tshisekedi. In 1990, Mobutu relented to the demands for reforms by lifting the ban on opposition activities in the country, but at the same time brutally suppressed the student uprising at the University of Lubumbashi, in which up to 150 students were killed. In 1991, Mobutu convened a national group that would prepare the country for a multiparty dispensation. The resulting Higher Council of the Republic (Haut

Conseil de la Republique, HCR), chose Etienne Tshisekedi as Prime Minister. His choice also reflected the importance Mobutu attached to the mineral-rich Kasai province where he hailed from.

Mobutu continued to undermine Tshisekedi using all kinds of maneuvers, including the army. To ensure the army's loyalty, he gave them carte blanche freedom to loot some regions, especially the mineral-rich eastern Congo. By 1994, Tshisekedi was so weakened that the opposition rallied behind Kengo wa Dondo as the new prime minister. Still, Mobutu dilly-dallied on the promised reforms, including the promised elections. During the late 1993 Rwanda invasion by the Rwandan Patriotic Front (RPF) forces of mainly Tutsi, against the Hutu-led government in Kigali, Mobutu made a strategic blunder of aligning himself with the latter, partly to regain favor with his former supporters, France, Belgium, and the US by offering them logistical support to intervene in Rwanda in support of the Hutu-led government. After the 1994 imbroglio that resulted in genocide which decimated the lives of an estimated one million mainly ethnic Tutsi and moderate Hutu Rwandese, Mobutu further provoked Rwanda with an attempt to expel the Banyamulenge, an ethnic Tutsi group from eastern Congo.

Opposition groups led by Laurent Desire Kabila's Alliance of Democratic Forces (Alliances des Forces Democratiques pour la Liberation du Congo-Zaire, AFDL), now joined by RPF, also sought, and obtained support from Uganda and Angola, whose dissident opposition had been supported by Mobutu. While an ailing Mobutu was in France in October 1996, seeking treatment for prostate cancer, Kabila's AFDL and his new allies launched a military offensive in the east of the country that captured Bukavu and Goma towns on Lake Kivu. Upon his return, Mobutu's army could not stop the advance of the rebels. By March 15, 1997, Kisangani City fell to the rebels, soon followed by the city of Mbuji Mayi. Efforts by the ANC government of South Africa to mediate a truce between the fighting forces failed miserably, and the rebels continued their blitzkrieg towards Kinshasha. The AFDL forces entered the capital on May 17, 1997, declaring Laurent Kabila the new president of the Republic of Congo. President Mobutu had fled to Morocco, where he died of cancer in Rabat, on September

7, 1997. In his final days, Mobutu had long abandoned his office and official residence in Kinshasha, for his chateau at Gbadolite. While in town, he occasionally operated from a luxury yacht anchored on the Congo River, between Kinshasha and Brazzaville.

Laurent Kabila's first action as president was to restore the country's old name of Congo, from Zaire, with a slight distinction (DRC), to distinguish it from Congo Brazzaville. At the time, he also had abundant goodwill from the international community, which hoped that anybody taking over the reins of power in Kinshasha, would either stop, or at least slow down the plunder and pilferage of the nation's resources. But as Kabila began to settle in office, later events would turn out to prove that he was just an illusion, with one Desire Kabila replacing another Desire Mobutu. Although he initiated steps for a new constitution to restore democracy, he tolerated no opposition, cramped down on public demonstrations, banned political parties, looted by the truckload, and effectively ruled by fiat. Pretty soon. He was accused of grossly violating human rights like his predecessor.

Ernesto (Che) Guevara, the Argentinian revolutionary who once fought alongside Fidel Castro in Cuba, had described Laurent Kabila in the least flattering colorful language in his diary, when the two rubbed shoulders in Congo's revolutionary wars in the early 60's.

He wrote,

"Kabila was a leader habitually unwilling to show his face at the front, spending his time, along with other Congolese leaders, in Cairo, Dar-es-Salaam and Paris, drinking Scotch in the best hotels in the company of beautiful women".

He continues,

"When in Kigoma, Tanzania, Kabila moved from saloon to whorehouse". He was, what was later referred to, as an "armchair revolutionary", issuing orders for others to carry out without his own participation.

As Laurent Kabila started getting comfortable on the job, he paid little attention to the demands of those that had helped him to capture power, especially Presidents Museveni and Kagame of Uganda and Rwanda, respectively. Both leaders had hoped that the new leadership in Kinshasha would effectively stop and even expel dissident opposition forces such as the ADF against Museveni, and remnants of the Interahamwe that had precipitated genocide in Rwanda. When their appeals to Kabila continued to fall on deaf ears, Kagame and Museveni collaborated, and aided by anti-Kabila elements in DRC, such as the Banyamulenge, they launched an offensive, turning their guns on their former comrade in arms, beginning August,1998.

By the end of 1998, in what would be dubbed as "Africa's World War", fighters from Uganda and Rwanda were pitied against Kabila's army, which was supported by troops from Angola, Namibia and Zimbabwe. The UN sent in peacekeepers, and initiated the Lusaka Peace Accords, which were signed by some but not others. Meantime, fighting continued to escalate, further complicated by ethnic divisions between groups such as the Hema and Lendu. The chaos in the eastern provinces also unleashed rivalries among hitherto comrades in arms that resulted in military exchanges between Uganda's UPDF and Rwanda's RPF in the city of Kisangani, on two separate occasions.

The unruly soldiers took turns in the wanton plunder of Congo's precious minerals, especially gold, diamonds and coltan (an essential ingredient in manufacturing cell phones). Truckloads of valuable mahogany and other hardwood timber became a common sight on Ugandan and Rwandan roads, some for domestic use, while others continued to Mombasa and Dar-es-Salaam ports, destined for the export market. These were illicit activities which drained Congo's resources, prompting Congo's government to sue Uganda at the International Court at The Hague, where a levy of $10 billion in Congo's favor was placed on Uganda, and still stands up to now.

In January 2001, President Laurent Kabila was assassinated, allegedly by his bodyguard, although many sources point to the fact that Kabila had acquired so many enemies in such a short time, that it was only a matter of time before any of these could have pulled the trigger. The elder Kabila was replaced by his son, Joseph, 28 years old at the time. The young president quickly embarked on reaching a peaceful settlement with the governments of Uganda and Rwanda. Both governments accepted a proposed pullout, which set the stage for negotiating a power-sharing agreement in Pretoria, South Africa, in December 2002. Both a transitional government as well as a new constitution were set up in April 2003, and later ratified in July, allowing Joseph Kabila to remain President. The UN sent in the largest contingent of peacekeepers ever, (20,000) as Congo's situation remained fragile.

Estimates of the death toll from Africa's world war range between 3-5 million, some directly caught up in crossfire, but the majority falling victim to hunger and debilitating diseases. Gross violations of human rights were rampant, some caused by local militia groups fighting to control their turf, while others were attributed to the so-called UN protectors in blue helmets, part of MONUC's large contingent of peacekeepers. Some of the atrocities committed defy description. Women and girls as young as three years old were repeatedly raped and traumatized by marauding soldiers, causing them irreparable damage to their mental and bodily physique.

The 2018 Nobel Peace Prize was awarded to two remarkable and most deserving individuals. Dr. Dennis Mukwege, a Congolese gynecologist works out of Panzi Hospital in Bukavu, in eastern Congo logging in 17-hour days performing repairs on women victims of rape, including fistula. The Globe and Mail describes Dr. Mukwege as perhaps, the world's leading expert on repairing injuries of rape. His co-recipient was Nadia Murad Basee Taha, an Iraqi Yazdi, who was captured on September 15, 2014, from her hometown of Kocho by soldiers of the Islamic State (ISIS) after killing 600 people in her village, including six of her own brothers. She was held and repeatedly raped for three months in Mosul, until she managed to escape after her captor carelessly left the door unlocked. She first settled in a refugee camp, and later found her way to Germany. She founded an organization called Nadia's Initiative, dedicated to helping women and children victimized by war and human trafficking.

President Joseph Kabila won two elections during his tenure, one in 2006, and the second in 2011. In both cases, he exploited the power of incumbency that at times allowed him to change the rules midstream, giving him extra advantages over his rivals. The second election in 2011 pitied Kabila against ten other candidates, the most prominent of whom was former prime Minister Etienne Tshisekedi. A January constitutional amendment had eliminated the need for a second round of voting for the top two vote-getters. This allowed Kabila to win over Tshisekedi with a simple majority of 49% versus 32% for the veteran politician. President Kabila was not eligible for a third electoral term under the prevailing constitution, so his term was supposed to end in November 2016.

But Kabila had become an excellent student of African Incumbency Politics, where a president never gives up power voluntarily, unless pushed to do so, no matter what the constitution says. As early as 2013, he had started showing tell-tell signs that he would not allow the scheduled elections to take place. In May 2016, the Constitutional Court ruled that if the scheduled elections were delayed, Kabila could stay in power until elections were held. Then, that September, the Electoral Commission formally requested the Constitutional Court to postpone the elections. Although this angered opposition groups, on December 31, 2016, the government struck a deal with them, brokered by the country's influential Catholic church. Under the arrangement, President Kabila would be allowed to remain in office until the next election, on an interim basis, with an opposition appointed prime minister.

Although the scheduled election date of November 2017 was missed, both internal and external pressure was kept on Kabila to step down. A new election date was set for December 23, 2018, but in August 2018, Kabila announced through his spokesman, that he would not participate in the forthcoming elections. Kabila threw his support behind Emmanuel Ramazani Shadary of the Peoples Party for Reconstruction and Democracy, (PPRD). Two prominent politicians had been eliminated by the Electoral Commission for various reasons. Jean-Pierre Bemba was denied participation on account of human rights charges he had faced at the International Criminal Court (ICC), while Moise Katumbi, a long-term adversary of Kabila, was embargoed for his long absence from the country.

The opposition first rallied behind Martin Fayulu, however, when supporters of Felix Tshisekedi staged protests, most withdrew their support for Fayulu, and instead backed the son of the late veteran politician who had died in Belgium in 2017. There were many attempts to interfere with the December 23 election, including a fire that burned electrical voting equipment in opposition strongholds. The Electoral Commission postponed the vote by a week to December 30 and delayed it up to March 2019 in violence-prone districts in the eastern part of the country. But, despite all the glitches, the election was held on December 30, 2018, and Felix Tshisekedi emerged victorious, garnering 38% of the vote. Fayulu who was favored to win by the polls scored 35%, took his allegations of fraud to court and lost. Ramazani, the government-sponsored candidate came up short, scoring only 24%.

On January 24, 2019, Felix Tshisekedi was inaugurated as Congo's duly elected president, marking the first peaceful transfer of power since independence in 1960. The elder Etienne Tshisekedi's remains were flown in from Brussels, and later laid to rest on June 1, 2019, in the presence of his son, also marking the end of an era that spanned nearly fifty years of political action. President Mobutu, despite his love for grandeur, was not afforded a similar sendoff in the country he dominated for 32 years. His bones are interred in a simple grave in a Moroccan cemetery, rather than a mausoleum in Kinshasha, or better still, his home base of Gbadolite as he would have wished.

The Democratic Republic of Congo (DRC), is a huge country, occupying an area of 2.345 million square kilometers. It is the largest sub-Saharan country and is only exceeded in size by Algeria on the African continent. Its estimated population of 77 million places it fourth, behind Nigeria (182 million), Ethiopia (103 million), and Egypt (89 million). The country is endowed with 80 million hectares of arable land, and an assortment of 1,100 different minerals, including gold, diamonds, copper, cobalt, and coltan, an essential ingredient in the manufacture of mobile phones. Oil deposits have also been discovered in the Albertine Graben bordering Uganda in the western Rift Valley area, although more work still needs to be done to determine the extent of the deposits.

The DRC's economy has always been hostage to the conflicts in the country since its independence. It took a particularly big hit following the prolonged conflicts stretching from 1997-2003, referred to as Africa's world war, from which it is yet to fully recover. This is because the conflicts were at the epicenter of the nation's mining activity in the eastern provinces, which forms the export base for the country. Copper and cobalt, both extracted from mines in the east, constitute close to 80% of the export revenue. Between 2015 and 2016, the nation's GDP growth dropped precipitously from 6.9% to 2.4%, the lowest performance since Joseph Kabila ascended to the presidency in 2001. An improvement in commodity prices pushed the growth rate up to 3.4%. However, a general downward trend in public revenue from 14.3% of GDP in 2014, to 8.2% of GDP in 2017, forced the government to curtail expenditures on public investment as well as social services.

Fiscal tightening, combined with export recovery helped push the current account deficit to 3.1% of GDP in 2017, down from 3.6% in 2016. Inflation was running as high as 54% in Fiscal 2017. The nation's debt burden stood at a manageable 17% of GDP during 2017, a dramatic fall from rates in excess of 100% in the 1990's.

On August 7, 2019, Gencore Mines announced that it would halt operations at its Mutanda Cobalt Mine, the world's largest. The move was prompted by a sharp drop in cobalt prices which have plummeted by nearly 40% in 2019. The company's setbacks include imposition of higher mining taxes in the country after a new code was passed by parliament. Gencore is also under scrutiny by the US Justice Department for its business practices in the DRC, as well as its relationship with Israeli Billionaire businessman Dan Gertler. The Mutanda mine produces a combination of copper and cobalt. In 2018, it produced 200,000 tons of copper, and 27,000 tons of cobalt, accounting for one fifth of the global production of cobalt. The metal is a critical component in the manufacture of lithium-ion batteries for electric cars. The company has halted and restarted operations before, following a sharp drop in prices. It will be placed in a care and maintenance status at the end of 2019.

The country suffers a chronic shortage of infrastructure for such a vast area. There are less than 3,000 kilometers of paved roads, and its railways are old, dilapidated and dangerously in need of replacement. But the recent successful and peaceful power transfer from Joseph Kabila to

Felix Tshisekedi at the beginning of 2019, the first since independence in 1960, brings a lot of optimism, that finally, the long-sleeping giant may be waking from its slumbers. On March 29, 2022, DRC joined the East African Community as its 7th member. As the largest country within the group, it will present a large untapped market potential, backed by an incredible mineral wealth. However, it remains saddled by the least developed infrastructure, constant bickering, and internecine violence, especially in the east which may hold it back from exploiting the benefits of joining the EAC.

CHAPTER 15

The tiny nation of Rwanda captured the attention of the whole world for nearly three months, beginning in April 1994, when Hutu forces known as Interahamwe (those who strike together), allied with the Rwandese national army, to avenge President Juvenal Habyarimana's death, and unleashed terror on mainly Tutsi and moderate Hutus, resulting in untold deaths. This genocide decimated 1,074,017 people, or nearly 12% of the population, according to a systemic count by the Rwandese government and survivor groups. Of these, 934,218 have been identified by name, and 93.6% were categorized as belonging to the Tutsi ethnic group. The world had not seen such atrocities since Adolf Hitler's Third Reich gassed nearly 6 million Jews, and Cambodia's Pol Pot slaughtered millions in his infamous Killing Fields in the 1970's.

The history of Rwanda has always been a powder keg. This small, central-African country sandwiched between Uganda to the north, DRC to the west, Burundi to the South, and touching Tanzania to the south-east, has a long history of ethnic clashes. Both Rwanda and Burundi, have the same ethnic composition, with the Hutu dominating at 85%, followed by the Tutsi at 14%, and a smattering of the semi-nomadic

Batwa at 1%. The two countries have a shared similar pattern of ethnic tensions, although Rwanda appears to have learned better lessons, following its tragedy with the 1994 genocide. During the scramble for Africa, following the Berlin Conference of 1884, Germany acquired the territory currently known as Rwanda and Burundi in 1899, to expand its East African possessions, which already included Tanganyika (Tanzania). But after Germany's defeat during the 1st World War, it was stripped of its possessions, the League of Nations handing Rwanda and Burundi to Belgium, while the administration of Tanganyika was taken over by the British.

The Tutsi had established a kingdom in Rwanda as early as the 16th century, with this minority pastoral tribe effectively ruling over, and subjugating the larger agrarian Hutu. Belgium which had also colonized Congo, the giant neighbor to the west, continued administering the two territories until 1959, basically using the same rudimentary formula they employed in the Congo. To effectively govern the feuding tribes, the Belgians accentuated their differences, highlighting such physical features as long thin noses (Tutsi), versus wide flat ones (Hutu), and even height. In meetings with Tutsi leaders, they would emphasize the group's superiority over the Hutu, while in another meeting with Hutu, they praised them for their agricultural prowess. The Belgians exploited these tribal differences, offering extra incentives to the ruling Tutsi, to crack the whip over non-conforming Hutu, so they alone could remain the arbiters.

Lack of opportunities among the majority Hutu, along with the restrictions imposed on them, created a lot of animosity towards the Belgians and the domineering Tutsi class, making a potential for clashes inevitable. By the time Rwanda agitated for independence along with other African countries, the internal war drums had been sounding not only against the Belgian colonizers, but against their Tutsi collaborators as well. In 1959, the Tutsi formed the Union Nationale Rwandaise to prepare for independence. In parallel fashion, the Hutu also formed Parti de l'emancipation du peuple Hutu (Parmehutu).

Prior to the elections of 1960, Parmehutu instigated a major uprising that resulted into the death of perhaps, thousands, of Tutsis. King Kigeri

V, along with thousands of Tutsis fled into exile in neighboring Uganda, others into Burundi. King Kigeri would be the last monarch Rwanda would ever have. In 1961, the monarchy was abolished, the country declared a republic, and Belgium granted Rwanda its independence on July 1, 1962. Gregoire Kayibanda became President of the country, and during his tenure, state-sponsored discrimination and violence against the Tutsi became de rigueur. The worst of these episodes came in 1963, after an incursion by Tutsi exiles from Burundi invaded Rwanda. In retaliation, angry Hutu vigilantes massacred as many as 15,000 Tutsis in the country, sending a wave of another exodus of refugees to neighboring countries.

My small village of Kabura is perhaps 100 miles north of the Rwandese border. But, as a kid in primary (elementary) school, in 1963, we used to see throngs of emaciated men, women and young children with spindly legs, swaying with their earthly possessions on their heads, probably heading towards government-designated refugee camps. One of these families, Mr. Mbarara, his wife Ndeti, mother-in-law Mukarutamu, and children Kalori and Maria, were welcomed and settled at our village catholic church. They were housed in a small grass-thatched hut, next to the catechist's house. Although not everyone in the village was thrilled to have them around, many in our village took on their plight very seriously. My father was one such a person. From the moment they settled, my father would make almost nightly visits to ensure that they were fed, and that they had the basic necessities of life, which at village level wasn't much. At home, my father, Mzee Tobi Ngazoire, gave us marching orders, to deliver raw food to the family, at least once every two or three days. Also, on important occasions such as Easter, the Mbarara family would be invited to share a meal with us, although verbal communication was a little difficult, since they spoke only Kinyarwanda, while we spoke Runyankore. But the children were about the same age, so we interacted very well, despite the linguistic differences.

There were no theaters or any such forms of entertainment in my village at the time (there are still none today). However, the Ministry of Information had established a unit called a "Traveling Theater", whereby the Ministry dispatched vans with movie projectors to entertain and educate the public in remote upcountry stations. One day, on our way home from school, we learned that the van was in our town of Rukungiri, and that there would be a show that evening. My elder brother and I, together with other students, decided to pitch camp and watch the movie. By the time the movie ended, it was dark, but we were all happy, and sang our way home. Arriving home, my father, who ordinarily would not be at home at such time, was calmly seated on his chair, holding his chin. My mom had just finished preparing the evening meal, and she was about to serve the food. We immediately smelled some trouble.

"You came home very late today, where have you been?", my father asked. He was only met with a mumble and a blank stare.

"Did any of you fetch firewood or water to make tonight's meal?", another blank stare. Then he dropped the other shoe.

"Who took food to Mbarara's family today?", he asked, although he already knew the answer. Little did we know that he had visited the family that evening and had delivered the food himself.

My father was the consummate disciplinarian who spared no rod. He kept one in his bedroom, which he occasionally used to straighten any of us who went astray. That night, he ordered us to lie down, and we each received about five strokes, plus a little jab if you objected. In addition, he ordered us to go to bed without dinner, to give us a sense of what it means sleeping on an empty stomach, a lesson I have carried with me since.

When my father passed away in 2004, Mr. Mbarara, then himself an old man with grandchildren, and settled in another village miles away, came with his family to attend the funeral. He appeared very distraught, and from his demeanor, one could discern, that he, too, had lost a father. During my secondary (high) school days at Kigezi College, Butobere, the student body had a sizeable proportion of immigrant students from Rwanda. The school is located in Kabale town, only about 25 kilometers from the Uganda-Rwanda border.

President Kayibanda remained at the helm in Kigali, until the army chief of staff, Maj-Gen Juvenal Habyarimana staged a coup that toppled him in 1973. Habyarimana ruled as a military strongman until the elections of 1977, after which a new constitution was promulgated in 1978, transforming him into a civilian president. In 1979, Rwandan exiles in the diaspora combined to form a party, the Rwandese Alliance for National Unity (RANU), whose main objective was to oppose the government's policies which favored perpetual domination by the Hutu, clamped on dissent, and discouraged dialogue. This same party metamorphosized in 1987, into the Rwanda Patriotic Front (RPF). The revamped party, like most liberation counterparts on the continent, had a military wing, the RPA, with the objective of changing the regime in Kigali militarily, if necessary. Most of the top military brass were Rwandese exiles living in Uganda, who had honed their military skills by helping President Museveni launch a successful guerilla offensive in 1981 that eventually toppled President Milton Obote in 1985. President Paul Kagame, had, for instance served as Museveni's chief of intelligence during the protracted warfare. Maj-Gen Fred Rwigema, who commanded the initial incursion by the RPA into Rwanda, and subsequently got killed by sniper fire on the second day, was also a top commander in Museveni's National Resistance Army (NRA). The RPA launched its invasion on October 1, 1990, with a lot of logistical and materiel support from Museveni's army. The Ugandan army lost hundreds of experienced military personnel who became part of the invading force of RPA.

The guerilla war dragged on from 1990 until April 6, 1994, when the presidential jet carrying Presidents Juvenal Habyarimana of Rwanda, and Cyprien Ntaryamira of Burundi was shot down as it descended to land at Kanombe International Airport in Kigali. Both presidents were Hutus, and they were returning from Dar-es-Salaam, where Habyarimana had just signed a power-sharing deal with RPA rebels. The Dassault Falcon 50 plane was brought down by surface-to-air missiles as it prepared to land. The actual shooter of the plane has never clearly been identified, although most conventional wisdom leaves very little doubt that the Tutsi rebels had everything to gain by eliminating Habyarimana. The counter argument to this theory is that Hutu hardliners downed the aircraft, in order to stop the power-sharing with Tutsis.

But, regardless of who shot the plane, the incident plunged Rwanda into its darkest hour, unleashing the evil forces of ethnic cleansing by Hutus over Tutsis, with a viciousness unlike any other time in their past conflagrations. It's been a quarter century since the end of the genocide in Rwanda, and yet, the world still cannot come to grips with the spirits that possessed one group of people to want to eliminate another from the surface of mother earth. The numbers are staggering and can leave anyone speechless. The government of Rwanda has put the total number of deaths at 1,074,017 people, or nearly 12% of the population. Nearly 94% of these were categorized as Tutsi. The rest are divided among moderate Hutus killed by fellow Hutus, and Hutus killed by Tutsis in revenge. The precision and speed at which this heinous exercise was carried out is astounding. It was all over in a mere 100 days. To put this in context, this is equivalent to the US government eliminating the entire African American population.

The downing of President Habyarimana's plane was only the spark plug that triggered the inferno, but not the actual cause. The entire episode had been pre-meditated and planned ahead of time by Hutu extremists. Tensions had been searing over generations. Every once-in-a-while, a situation arose that sparked off a scuffle, but never on this scale. Rwanda is a Maryland sized country with three ethnic groups that had lived in relative harmony for centuries before Germany colonized after the Berlin Conference of 1884. German rule ended in 1918 after its defeat in the First World War, and its Central African territories, including Rwanda and Burundi, were transferred to Belgium by the League of Nations. But neither Germany, nor Belgium wished to station a large contingent of troops in Rwanda to maintain order. Instead, they allied themselves with the ruling class of Tutsis, by arming them, and emphasizing their superiority over the majority Hutus.

The social concept known as Ubuhake/Obuhuku created a feudal system where the poor peasant class of Hutus worked as indentured servants for the wealthier Tutsi, in exchange for a cow further widening the gap between the ethnic groups. The Belgians created artificial barriers between the groups, which further drove a wedge among them. And, for a small land-locked country with limited resources, whatever opportunities became available, the Belgians seemed to give favor to the Tutsis. For instance, the political and economic reforms the Belgians instituted between the 1920's and the 1930's, to integrate indigenous Rwandans, only helped to consolidate and entrench Tutsi power. The Tutsis in turn, cracked the whip on their compatriots in order to please their mentors. But for the Hutu, these lopsided developments became the building blocks to an inevitable revolution against both the Belgians and their surrogate Tutsi oppressors.

The onslaught of genocide began in earnest on April 7, 1994, a day after the presidential plane was brought down by a surface-to-air missile, killing everyone aboard. The RPF guerilla war into Rwanda had been halted by a UN peace agreement initiated in August 1993 between the RPF rebels and President Habyarimana's Hutu-led government. However, there were elements on both sides for whom power-sharing was anathema. These sentiments were stronger on the Hutu side, who even considered Habyarimana's signing of an agreement with the rebels, a betrayal. Their ultimate solution was to totally obliterate the "inyenze" (cockroaches), as the Tutsis were referred to.

As early as January 1994, the UN contingent observer force under Canadian General Romeo Dallaire, was sending sos messages to the late Kofi Annan, then head of Peacekeeping at the UN in New York. The main message was that Hutu extremists were arming themselves with machetes for an offensive against the Tutsi, but the messages were mostly ignored. The Clinton Administration even went so far as discouraging further troop deployment by the Security Council, to buttress those already on the ground. As Former President Clinton put it, it was, and remains the most regrettable decisions of his presidency.

Once the slaughter started on April 7, 1994, the marauding gangs executed it with brutal efficiency, killing an estimated 8,000, mostly Tutsi per day. The propaganda was orchestrated daily in the media by Radio & Television Libre des Mille Collines, which implored the Interahamwe to "exterminate the inyenze". The brutality and scale were of such a magnitude not seen anywhere since the Nazis death camps at

Auschwitz, and Pol Pot's killing fields of Cambodia. Stories abound of even Hutu husbands killing their Tutsi wives as part of the cleansing. When the actual killing started, both the UN and Belgians withdrew their forces, leaving the victims completely defenseless. The smell of death was everywhere, as bodies couldn't be cleared fast enough. The Akagera River, which is a tributary of Lake Victoria, became a dumping ground for dead bodies. Fishermen in Uganda soon abandoned their livelihood, scared by the number of bodies floating in the lake, and customers refusing to buy fish fed on human flesh.

It is often said that every dark cloud has a silver lining. In Steven Spielberg's Academy Award-winning Schindler's List, Liam Neeson plays Oskar Schindler a German industrialist, and a member of the Nazi Party who saved 1,200 lives of ghetto Jews by employing them in his enamelware and ammunitions factories in the occupied Polish protectorates of Bohemia and Moravia. Needless to mention that Schindler had joined the Nazi Party, and later protected the Jews out of expediency to keep his business enterprise going.

Out of the macabre situation in Rwanda, another hero emerged. Paul Rusesabagina, an ethnic Hutu, with a Tutsi wife, was a manager of Hotel des Milles Collines in Kigali Rwanda when all hell broke loose. In the ensuing chaos, he hid and saved 1,200 Hutus and Tutsis running to escape the wrath of the Interahamwe. He was later cast in the Academy nominated hit movie Hotel Rwanda, with Actor Don Cheadle playing his role. Paul has since been honored with many awards, including the US Presidential Medal of Freedom, Immortal Chaplains Prize for Humanity, the Wallenberg Medal of the University of Michigan, and dozens of others. It's not clear that Rusesabagina had anything to gain out of his actions, other than being driven by what Bishop Desmond Tutu of South Africa called "Ubuntu spirit", that uniqueness which separates a human being from an animal. He spends his time commuting between his homes in Brussels, Belgium, Houston Texas, where he has established the Paul Rusesabagina Humanitarian Foundation.

Forced into this untenable situation, the RPF, commanded by Maj-Gen Paul Kagame, fought fearlessly to defeat the perpetrators, and defend their own. It took 100 days to defeat the government forces and capture the capital, Kigali, forcing the Interahamwe to scamper for cover mostly into the jungles of the Democratic Republic of Congo. Kagame's army would later chase them there, leaving a trail of revenge killings of their own. Kagame's record on human rights has been mixed at best. The RPA was cited for gross human rights violations in many instances by organizations such as Amnesty International, the New York Times, Voice of America, the BBC, and others. In his book, Africa: A continent for the taking, veteran Journalist Howard W. French of the New York Times, follows the Trail of Tears from Rwanda into the wet and humid jungles of the ever-chaotic Democratic Republic of Congo. There, heavily armed battalions of the RPA hunt for remnants of the Interahamwe on a search-and-destroy mission, accompanied by a complete cover up of the evidence. It should be noted that the actions of the RPA in the DRC, precipitated what later turned into Africa's world war.

When Kagame first appeared on the scene in 1994, he was rather subdued and constrained in his approach, cognizant of the volatile race relations in Rwanda. Instead of the "winner-take-all" approach that's typical of victorious guerilla wars, he allowed Pasteur Bizimungu, a moderate Hutu to assume the presidency. He took the number two spot of Vice-President, which he combined with the Defense portfolio, making him the de facto ruler who called the shots. This delicate dance went on until 2000 when Kagame fell out with Bizimungu, ousted him, jailed him temporarily, before installing himself as president in 2001. The country promulgated a new more inclusive constitution and organized an election in 2010, which Kagame's RPF party won overwhelmingly, legitimizing him as a civilian president. However, from the start, the power structure once again favored the Tutsi, who controlled both the economy and the military establishment. In 2015, a constitutional amendment was inserted, allowing Kagame to rule until 2034. In a closely controlled election, he won another 7-year term in 2017 by a landslide. But his penchant for intolerance to dissent is legendary. One of Kigali's most prominent business moguls, Mr. Tribert Rujugiro Ayabatwa, who financed the RPA when it was still a rag-tag guerilla force, was unceremoniously kicked out of the country, and his businesses, including the city's pre-eminent mall, seized by government. Many former senior RPA officers, such as Lt-Gen Faustin Kayumba Nyamwasa, once very close to Kagame, have been swept aside. Some have been jailed internally, while others were forced into exile. Kagame's hitmen have been known to follow and hound his detractors wherever they are, as happened in the case of former intelligence chief Patrick Karegeya. He was followed into his exile in South Africa, and strangled in his room on December 31, 2013, at the Michelangelo Towers Hotel in Sandton, an upscale suburb of Johannesburg, South Africa. Even the hero of Hotel Rwanda, Paul Rusesabagina was not spared. It appears that the fame and plaudits he earned by his actions, tickled the man who believes he should be the only bull in the kraal, the wrong way. When attempts by the RPF to belittle his noble contribution failed to get traction, he too, was forced into exile to Brussels, where he continued to be harangued by the regime in Kigali. They did not stop at that. Kagame engineered a scheme in which Rusesabagina's former friends lured him to attend a conference in neighboring Burundi. Once he fell for the bait, they monitored his flight schedule, captured him in Dubai, UAE, bound him onto a private jet, and flew him to Kigali. Once in their hands, they rushed him through a kangaroo court, charged hm with the most egregious crimes, including murder, and the judge sentenced him to life imprisonment, despite being a citizen of Belgium. International intervention has so far failed to have the Kagame regime extradite him to Belgium, or even to the US, where he once received accolades with a Congressional Medal of Honor.

None of this appears to have tarnished Paul Kagame's standing as one of Africa's feted Statesmen. He continues to jet from one capital to another, including his attendance of Queen Elizabeth II's funeral in London on September 19, followed by an address at the United Nations General Assembly in New York immediately afterwards. Former British Prime Minister Tony Blair has been Kagame's trusted advisor for a long time.

Economically, Rwanda benefitted from the goodwill of the international community, and Kagame, to his credit, took many pragmatic steps to rebuild a shattered nation. His steady hand has allowed Kigali, the capital, to be one of the few organized and functional cities on the continent, making the land of a thousand hills a favorite place for conventions. But his stranglehold on the political process, allowing Tutsi domination once again, makes Rwanda's future rather precarious and unsustainable. The country's economy registered a phenomenally high growth rate of 7.5% for the decade between 2008 and 2018, allowing per capita GDP to grow by an average 4.7% annually. Rwanda has built a reputation as a non-corrupt environment to do business, and its overall Economic Freedom index of 71.1 in 2019 lands it at number 32 in the world. This places it among the top echelons on the continent. But Rwanda's high growth was mainly driven by public investment, which has slowed down since 2017. Although authorities would like the private sector to drive economic growth going forward, low domestic savings, a skills gap, and the high cost of energy will continue constraining the economy. As a land-locked small country, high transport costs continue to have a serious impact on its agrarian economy. The Standard Gauge Railway (SGR), linking Rwanda to the Indian Ocean port of Mombasa through Kenya and Uganda has stalled due to lack of financing. The traditional route by truck through Uganda was closed from February 2019 to early 2022, over political and other personality differences between President Museveni and Kagame. It was only during the second half of August 2021, that an agreement to re-open it was signed in Luanda, the Angolan capital, thanks to President Joao Loulenco's mediation efforts. Although Presidents Kagame and Museveni of Uganda seem to have kissed and toned down their egos, suspicions of each other remain deep, and those familiar with both personalities know that a repeat performance could happen at any time, should one threaten the other's interests. This has forced Kigali to explore the possibility of an alternate route through Tanzania. Internally, perhaps the most significant thing Kagame has done was to empower women. At 64%, Rwanda has the highest percentage of female legislators in the world.

CHAPTER 16

The first Englishman to set foot in Uganda was John Hanning Speke in 1862. However, it took British-American explorer Henry Morton Stanley's letter, published in the London Daily Telegraph newspaper in 1875, to arouse and provoke interest in the British government into getting a piece of territory in that part of Africa. Two years later, in 1877, the first batch of Church Missionary Society (CMS) arrived in the country, to be followed by French Catholic missionaries in 1879. Thereafter, for the next 83 years until 1962, when Uganda got its independence, its course would be influenced and determined by foreign elements, primarily, the British.

When the Europeans first arrived in the country, they found society organized with well-established monarchies. The kingdoms had structures such as Lukiiko (parliament), Katikkiro, (prime minister) and a standing army to defend territory. Some, such as Bunyoro-Kitara and Buganda, had been bitter rivals for generations. The British would later exploit these divisions, and create other artificial barriers in society, where there were none before, in order to govern a fractured society. To counter the spread of Islam, and influence of Arabs who had preceded them, having arrived there in the 1840's, it was deemed necessary to immediately spread Christianity. But the kings were absolute monarchs who held sway over their subjects. Therefore, this top-down approach meant that to influence society, the king or chief had to be convinced first.

The Arabs had arrived with an agenda of spreading Islam, trading in ivory, precious metals and slaves, while the British anti-slavery movement wanted to establish Christianity and gain a foothold to halt slavery. The Kabaka (king) of Buganda, was thrust in the middle of these competing, and more often diverging priorities of the foreign elements, forcing him to switch allegiances from one camp to another. In 1886, when the European missionaries undermined Kabaka Mwanga II by converting his pages to Christianity to defy his authority, the infuriated monarch ordered 45 of the youthful pages to be burned alive at Namugongo. Of these, 22 were Catholic, while 23 were protestant. The location, about 8 miles north-east of Kampala City, is today, an international Christian pilgrimage site with a Martyrs shrine that has been visited by three reigning pontiffs, Pope Paul VI (1969) Pope John Paul II (1993), and Pope Francis (2015). Millions of the faithful from all walks of life flock there on June 3 of every year, to renew their faith, some after having walked long stretches, including crossing international borders.

In 1890, Britain and Germany signed a treaty which would give Britain the rights to take over the territory that would be known as Uganda. The same year, Captain Frederick Lugard, an agent of the Imperial British East African Company arrived in Uganda after enduring a treacherous 800-mile route from Mombasa on the Kenyan coast. Buganda was going through a lot of acrimony resulting from a society divided by foreign religious influences. Lugard set out to win Kabaka Mwanga II' s favor, sometimes driving hard bargains, in the presence of his troops with his famous Maxim guns. He prevailed, and won the treaty of allegiance from the Kabaka, paving the way to the creation of Uganda as a protectorate. Among his enduring legacies was the installation of protestant chiefs, whose influence over the Buganda Kingdom and other regions continues to-date. In 1894, Uganda became a protectorate.

Kabaka Mwanga II's position became untenable after he began persecuting Christians, especially after his order to burn his pages alive. The British CMS missionaries loathed him. The French Catholic missionaries led by Father Simeon Lourdel (Mapera) also sidelined him, while the Arab influence had long waned after he refused to be circumcised and instead got baptized with the name Danieli. In frustration with all foreign influences, he joined forces with his erstwhile foe, the Omukama Kabalega of Bunyoro-Kitara, who already had an ax to grind against the British.

The capture of Kabalega and Mwanga was an epoch period that marked a turning point for the success of British colonialism in Uganda. Although both monarchs had become major stumbling blocks in the colonization process, it was mainly Kabalega who was targeted, and whose capture was a coveted prize. All along, Kabalega was the most persistent and formidable of the Ugandan kings to reject foreign intrusion. Mwanga had only half-heartedly joined him as a last-ditch effort to safeguard his position after being threatened by all foreign religious elements following the execution of his pages. Kabalega had even previously backed Kiweewa, Mwanga's brother, as Kabaka, when Mwanga was temporarily exiled to Bulingugwe Island in Lake Victoria after refusing to be circumcised and converted into Islam. Mwanga's move to Bunyoro was prompted by the refusal of his top war architect, Gabudyeri Kintu to move there with him. As he could not face British troops alone, he ended up dividing his fighting force into two.

In March 1898, the British brought in some reinforcements from the 27th Bombay Light Infantry, which helped to disarm Kabalega's Sudanese mercenaries. This smoothed the way for launching a serious offensive against the rebel kings. For five years before, Kabalega had mobilized rebel soldiers, including Nubians and Somalis, against British installations. Even after their defeat by the British, the Sudanese continued their guerilla activities, until their leader Bilal Amin was killed. Following their leader's demise, they lost their fighting spirit, leaving Kabalega and Mwanga to their own devices. The British took advantage of these missteps by the rebels, so that by the end of 1898, they had gained the upper hand. But the rebels were still at large, sheltered by Langi collaborators in the swamps of Lake Kyoga. Then on April 9, 1899, the two kings were betrayed by their Langi and Bakedi allies. In a feat of irony, they were captured by two Baganda military collaborators of the British. Semei Kakungulu, a brother-in-law to Mwanga, apprehended Kabalega after he was shot in the arm. Mwanga was taken prisoner by Andrea Luwandaga, a perfect blend of divide and rule. However, despite his agony and predicament, Kabalega remained defiant to the end. Under the knife of the British Army surgeon who amputated his shattered arm, presumably without anesthesia, Kabalega cynically remarked, "I suppose you'll want to cut off the other arm, and probably my legs too".

The British exiled them to the Seychelles islands in the Indian Ocean, where Mwanga II died on May 8, 1903, at the age of 35. Kabalega was allowed to return home after 24 years but died in the eastern Ugandan town of Jinja in 1923, on his way home.

In 1896, the British embarked on building the Uganda Railway, a project that proved strategic during the early period of the scramble for Africa. The 1,000 mm (3ft 31/8 in) single track railway originally stretched from Mombasa on the Indian Ocean to Kisumu on the shores of Lake Victoria, for a total of 1,060 km (660 mi). It was later extended to cover the broad width of Uganda, from Tororo on the Kenyan border, to Kasese on the foothills of the Rwenzori Mountains. The man put in charge of this mega project was George Whitehouse, an experienced civil engineer who had worked on building railways in other British colonies such as India. Most of the construction workers or coolies were sourced from the Punjab area, and sent to Karachi, from where they were shipped to East Africa on steamers belonging to the British India Steam Navigation Company.

A total of 36,811 coolies signed contracts to work on the Uganda Railway between December 1895 and March 1901, when the first batch started returning to India. Over 6,700 coolies chose to stay, creating the foundational base of the now sizeable Indian community in East Africa.

While the workers faced many challenges endangering their lives, such as malaria, and marauding Maasai warriors opposed to the project, none frightened them more than a pair of lions, dubbed "The man-eaters of Tsavo". In 1898, during the construction of a bridge across the river Tsavo in what is today, known as Tsavo National Park, a pair of vicious mane-less male lions terrorized the workers by snatching and devouring one or two people a night, until they were hunted down and shot by Lt-Col John Henry Patterson. The total number of people killed and eaten by these beasts is put as high as 135. The lions' skins were used as house rugs by Patterson, until persuaded to sell them to the Chicago Field Museum, where the animals were reconstructed and are now on display. This author visited the Chicago-based Museum a while back, where he bore witness to these mass murderers. With no statute of limitations on murder, one hopes the Kenyan authorities will continue pursuing the fugitives for extradition, to face their day in court over atrocities committed nearly a century and a half ago. During the inauguration of President Barack Obama in January 2009, this author chanced upon a delegation from Kenya, who had come to attend their famous cousin's investiture to the White House in Washington DC. Among them, was a gentleman who professed to be on a mission to return these runaway fugitives back to Kenya. The fellow even garnered an interview on the Oprah Winfrey show to argue his case. It would appear the Field Museum continues to abet with the criminals up to now, since they are still hiding there.

For his transgressions against British rule, Kabaka Mwanga II was deposed by a Council of Chiefs led by Katikkiro Apollo Kaggwa on August 9, 1897. The deposed king had two wives with young male children, both of whom were potential heirs, but the raging rivalry between Catholics and Protestants would play a role in which child would become the next Kabaka. Stanislas Mugwanya and the catholic chiefs kidnapped the catholic wife, while the protestant chiefs led by Apollo Kaggwa held the protestant one. To the protestants' luck. The catholic child died in infancy, leaving the 13-month-old Daudi Chwa II to be crowned as Buganda's youngest Kabaka on August 14, 1897. The chiefs would remain as Regents until the young monarch became of age. Then in 1900, Britain and Buganda signed the Buganda Agreement that established Buganda as a constitutional monarchy. More treaties were signed between the British and the rulers of other kingdoms including

Ankole, Toro, and Bunyoro, expanding the territory that now constitutes Uganda. A small portion of Eastern Uganda, extending into Nyanza province was ceded to Kenya in 1902. This region of Kenya happens to be the one where former President Obama's ancestors hailed from.

As the British empire expanded, so was the cost of running it. During Captain Lugard's stint in Uganda, the colonial office considered the possibility of abandoning their presence in the country due to the increasing cost of administering the territory. Lugard had to make a quick trip to London, to plead and convince his bosses that the experiment was worthwhile. One way the British chose to defray the costs, was to introduce cash crops. Among the cash crops introduced in the early 1900's were cotton, coffee, and tea. These would primarily be grown by peasant farmers, selling their crops to Indian merchants, who would then export the merchandise to generate income that the government could tax for revenue. Peasants had a poll tax imposed on each head of family to force them to grow the crops.

The trouble with this economic model was that it created a lopsided exploitative class, with Indian merchants who paid farmers extremely low prices, irrespective of what the crops fetched on the world markets. The colonial administrators, in cahoots with the Indian merchants did everything possible to put hurdles that prevented indigenous Africans from participating directly in trade without Indian middlemen. It was issues such as these, that later formed the basis for President Idi Amin's policy of summarily expelling the Indian merchants from Uganda beginning September 1972. The cash crop distribution in the early stages, was concentrated in the central region of Buganda, partly to reward Baganda chiefs for their cooperation with the colonial administrators. Over the years, this has created a large income differential among the four main regions of the country, led by Buganda at the top, and northern Uganda at the tail end.

Commercial farming, especially in sugarcane and tea was gradually introduced by a small Indian merchant class, led by Muljibhai Prabhudas Madhvani, the scion of the Madhvani Group of Kakira Sugar Industries, in Jinja, and the Mehta Group of Lugazi, in Mukono district. Coffee production, which, for the longest period of modern Uganda's existence, was the largest export earner, remained in the hands of smallholder producers, although there has been some sort of a geographical shift in its production, away from Buganda to the Western and Eastern regions. Tea estate farming has been practiced for several decades, led by people like the late Amirali Kamali, the head of the Mukwano Conglomerate who died in Kampala on July 11, 2019. Of late, other crops such as bananas, pineapples and rice have been undertaken on a commercial basis, this time, by indigenous Ugandan farmers.

Although Uganda's Legislative Council (LEGICO) was established in 1921, it only allowed Europeans and Indians to participate. The first African members were admitted in 1945.They were Michael Ernest Kawalya Kaggwa, Katikkiro of Buganda, Petero Nyangabyaki, Omuhanika (Prime Minister) of Bunyoro, and Yekoniya Zirabamuzale, Secretary General of Busoga. That same year saw what came to be referred to as the Buganda Riots. The participants put out a list of demands, including, (1), the right to bypass price controls on export sales, (2) removal of monopoly of cotton ginning by Indians, (3) the right to elect their own representatives instead of puppet chiefs. The colonial administrators thought these demands were instigated by supporters of communism. One of the leaders of the riot group was a firebrand by the name of Ignatius Kangave Musazi. Among the actions they took during the riots, was burning down the homes of the pro-colonial supporters. The riots were on and off between 1945-49. Sir John Hathorn Hall who was Governor of the country from 1945-52, dismissed and rejected these demands as communist antics. Mr. Musazi had formed Uganda African Farmers Union (UAFU) as early as 1947, which the governor banned in 1949, blaming it for the riots.

Mr. Musazi's role in the anti-colonial movement and building Uganda's political foundation cannot be over-emphasized. Born in a small village called Timuna, near Wobulenzi in present Luwero District, he attended Kings College Budo, later gaining a scholarship to study Divinity in the UK. In 1936, he met and married Mary Ritah Nansinkombi, the grand-daughter of Sir Apollo Kaggwa, the turn-of-the century Buganda Prime Minister. But, unlike other western-educated elites such as Namdi Azikiwe of Nigeria, or Nkrumah of Ghana, whose countrywide nationalism were above reproach, the early elites in Uganda were concentrated in Buganda, with an ambivalent approach that favored Buganda, rather than Uganda. To channel farmers' grievances towards the colonial administration, in 1938, for instance, Musazi and other elites formed a group known as Bazukkulu ba Kintu (grandchildren of Kintu).

However, with the advent of WW II in 1939, the British recruited many youths from all parts of the country, exposing them to experiences and cultures beyond their own. It is estimated that out of the 533,084 Africans who directly participated during the 5-year war effort, 76,166 were drawn from Uganda. These soldiers returned home with new attitudes towards colonialism, some having witnessed first-hand, how the British advocated fighting for democracy, while denying the basic tenets of it in the colonies. The war also introduced another element that favored decolonization in the form of the bi-polar world of the cold war, with the US championing the free world, while the Soviet Union led the socialist camp. Upon their return at the end of the war, more Africans under colonialism began to demand higher participation in determining their own destiny. In Kenya, British colonial attitudes towards the country changed with the emergence of the Mau Mau Resistance in 1952, which raised the stakes of retaining territory and protecting their citizens in the new colony. Meantime, in Uganda that year, Sir Andrew Cohen, a more liberal governor, took over from Sir John Hall. Cohen formed a commission that investigated the farmers' grievances, creating an atmosphere that later allowed Musazi, and other colleagues like Abubakar Mayanja and Apollo Kironde, to form the Uganda National Congress party. The UNC, like the Uganda African Farmers Union (UAFU) banned by Governor John Hall, was formed to address economic welfare issues related to exploitation of African farmers by Indian merchants, and poor-to-nonexistent political representation. The party's ideological orientation was socialist, under the tutelage of Fenner Brokway, a socialist Labor Party Member of the British Parliament, together with another socialist named John Stonehouse, who organized the farmers' cooperative movement. Musazi also solicited help from George Shepherd, an American Ph D student at the London School of Economics, who spent two years in Uganda helping with the infrastructural setup of the party.

The UNC's socialist orientation put it on a collision course with the colonial administration, bent on halting the spread of communism in its tracks. For that reason, the government encouraged other small parties to grow in competition with UNC, while at the same time fomenting the growth of splinter groups from within. Among the people who played a role, and later benefitted from the disintegration of UNC was Apollo Milton Obote. He would later become one of the key-players towards Uganda's independence. After being expelled from Makerere University in the late 1940's, Obote had moved to Kenya, where he worked with the Trade Unions, and participated in the anti-colonial movement, including membership in the Kenya African Union which was on the rise there. He returned to Uganda in 1956 and was soon elected to represent his Lango District in the Legco, replacing a low-key politician called Yakobo Omonya. His election had been under the umbrella of UNC.

Once in the Legco, he used his eloquence effectively, and was soon considered one of the strongest advocates of the anti-colonial movement. Within the UNC itself, Obote was among the strongest opponents of the parochial view favored mainly by Baganda, of giving Buganda a special status, rather than an equal position within the national context of Uganda. He had taken his Legco seat in March 1958, and by December of the same year, the UNC split into two factions, the smaller group being known as the Uganda Peoples Union (UPU). Obote remained in the UNC. Soon, however, the party would face a crisis emanating from doctrine differences among its founders. The young cohort favored party policies that were in tune with the Pan-African movement, represented by firebrands like John Kalekyezi (father of former Inspector General of Police, Kale Kayihura). The party had established an office in Cairo, Egypt, where Kalekyezi coordinated its activities with those of other anti-colonial movements. The more conservative members of the UNC, including Musazi, were opposed to the role played by this office.

The real crisis came to a head after three senior party members of

UNC, Abu Mayanja, Jolly Joe Kiwanuka, and Dr Kununka returned from a Pan-African conference in Accra in December 1958, making a stop in Cairo. Upon their return, they defended the role of the Cairo office, as that of keeping Uganda from isolationism, and more in tune with emerging nationalism everywhere. Musazi, then president of the party, called this heresy, and made a move to expel six of the leaders subscribing to this ideology. In the end, it was Musazi himself who was expelled. Milton Obote was elected president to replace him. Soon after that, Obote's wing of the UNC merged with the Uganda Peoples Union, creating the Uganda Peoples' Congress (UPC), which would lead the country to independence on October 9, 1962.

Another luminary and towering figure of the independence era was Benedicto Kagimu Mugumba Kiwanuka. Born May 11, 1922, in Bukomansimbi, Masaka District. He received his primary education in Masaka, after which he attended St. Peters Secondary School, Nsambya. During the 2nd WW, he was recruited into the Kings African Rifles (KAR), ending up serving as a sergeant in Palestine. Upon his return after the war, he took a job as a library attendant at the Uganda High Court. This was during the period of the Buganda Riots of 1945-49. The colonial government had arrested some of the rioters, accusing them of masterminding the destruction of properties belonging to supporters of the government, (mainly chiefs). The rioters had hired an American defense lawyer to represent them. While doing research about the case at the library, he solicited help from the young library attendant, whom he found well-organized and competent. He encouraged him to further his education, stimulating his interest in the legal profession.

With few facilities available to him in Uganda at the time, Kiwanuka ended up enrolling at Pope Pius X College in Maseru, Basutoland (Lesotho). During his stay there, he heard many horrendous stories of economic and social injustice, narrated by classmates from other colonies, especially those ruled by white supremacists in countries like Southern Rhodesia (Zimbabwe) and South Africa. The stories formed the basis of his commitment to fight for justice everywhere. Proceeding to Law School in London, he was admitted to Grey's Inn, where he would train as a barrister. While in London, the Kabaka of

Buganda, Sir Edward Mutesa II was deposed and exiled to London in 1953. Kiwanuka, by now prominent among the Ugandan student community in London, volunteered his legal services to the Buganda delegation led by Justice Matayo Mugwanya in arguing the case against the displacement of the Kabaka. The Kabaka returned to his throne in 1955.

Mugwanya became president of the Democratic Party, but when Kiwanuka returned to the country in 1956, the leadership of the party organized a big welcome bash, at which Mugwanya proclaimed that, "ensi eno tugikulaamidde", meaning, we entrust this country to you. Kiwanuka who had set up a private legal practice, Kiwanuka & Co Advocates, combined his legal practice with active participation in DP party activities. In 1958, he was overwhelmingly elected as president of the party. By then, the country's political establishment was in the ring, agitating for independence like many others on the continent.

The two oldest parties in the country, the Democratic Party (DP), and Uganda Peoples' Congress (UPC), trace their foundations to the two main religious affiliations of Catholicism and Anglicanism, respectively. Both parties have their roots in Buganda, where European missionaries first introduced the foreign religions. Upon establishing a protectorate, the British introduced a system of indirect rule through chiefs, whom they converted to Anglican Protestantism, which ultimately became the faith of the ruling elite. But the French had introduced Catholicism to Buganda at about the same time, which was widely embraced by the rank and file. This created a gap between the two groups, in which the protestants benefitted more from the largess of the Kabaka and his chieftainship. Over the years, this manifested itself into resentment and a sort of disloyalty towards the Kabakaship. The DP was formed to unite Baganda Catholics, who not only wanted to fight foreign domination under colonialism, but also internal domination of the ruling class in equal measure.

Milton Obote's UPC was created out of a merger between an offshoot of the UNC and UPU, both of which were based in Buganda. These were led by protestant elites affiliated with Mengo, the seat of the Kabaka. Obote's major impact was to expand the party beyond the confines of Buganda, to embrace membership from other regions. However, this faced resistance from the Baganda, who considered this as an affront towards usurping power from the center. Therefore, as the parties campaigned on their manifestos to lead the country to independence, Baganda elites had to make a choice between Catholic prodigal son Ben Kiwanuka, or Milton Obote, a northerner, but a fellow Anglican. During the elections of 1961, after the British extended Uganda self-governing status, Kiwanuka prevailed, making him the country's first Prime Minister. But in the April 1962 general elections, Buganda, which by now had created another party of royalists known as Kabaka Yekka (king only), chose to align Kabaka Yekka with UPC. Obote took the reins of power of an independent Uganda on October 9, 1962, as Executive Prime Minister, while Sir Edward Mutesa II, the Kabaka of Buganda, became ceremonial president.

This marriage of convenience between UPC and Kabaka Yekka lasted until May 22, 1966. On that day of infamy, Obote, on suspicions that the Kabaka was stocking arms and undermining his authority using a foreign power (presumed to be Britain), ordered a battalion of Uganda Army to invade the Kabaka's Lubiri (palace) at Mengo, with the intention of searching for the rumored cache of arms stored there. Sir Freddie, as the Kabaka was popularly called, got wind of the impending invasion through his royalist insiders, buying him time to escape capture. But the invasion only marked the culmination of a settlement of scores within the ruling party, which had started three months earlier on February 22. Obote's egalitarian approach to society had never hidden his disdain for the royalists among the ruling party members who wanted Buganda to retain a special status above the other regions. Although it was Buganda that irked him most, to him, hereditary rulers, all of whom were concentrated in the south (Buganda, Bunyoro, Toro and Ankole), paused a permanent barrier towards uniting the Bantu of the south, and the Nilotics of the north.

Earlier, in 1963, the Buganda Lukiiko (parliament), had threatened to withdraw Buganda's cooperation with the central government if the latter did not remove all its police stations from Buganda. This clash had been triggered by the central government's refusal to fund the budget in

Buganda. Some disgruntled elements in the Buganda Lukiiko had taken it a step further, suggesting that Obote should remove his entire central government from Buganda territory and run it elsewhere. Matters were not helped by Obote's refusal to allow the Army band to play at the Kabaka's birthday, which he called a non-national event, but which the Baganda considered an insult to the Kabaka. Besides Buganda, there was rivalry between Obote and up-and-coming ambitious members of the UPC party such as John Kakonge, the Secretary, and Grace Ibingira, the legal advisor. After Kakonge was ousted and replaced by Ibingira, a royalist from Ankole Kingdom, Obote's rivalry against him only increased, reaching a crescendo when Ibingira used his brother, Major Katabarwa to launch a coup-attempt which failed to remove Obote. Grace Ibingira, along with four other cabinet ministers were arrested, thrown into "the University by the lake" (Luzira Prison), where they would languish until Idi Amin released them after overthrowing Obote in January 1971. That action sealed the fate of Uganda's kingdoms which Obote dissolved with the 1967 Republican constitution.

The saga created what would be referred to as the Buganda Crisis, (Bisela bya Kabenge), which put an indelible mark between Obote and Buganda, that haunted him until his death in a Johannesburg hospital on October 10, 2005. After the assault on Lubiri, Obote abrogated the 1962 constitution, and, with help from his Attorney General, Godfrey Binaisa, created what came to be known as the "pigeonhole" constitution. With it, among other things, Obote created the position of Executive President for himself, and declared Uganda a Republic, after abolishing all kingdoms and hereditary rulers.

Obote's snake-and-frog dance with Buganda continued to get worse after he declared an emergency over Buganda. In1969, Kabaka Mutesa II died in his London apartment under suspicious circumstances after meeting a Ugandan woman. Obote himself survived an attempted assassination at Lugogo Stadium that drove a bullet through his jaw, knocking out a few teeth. After the incident, all opposition parties, including DP, the main one, were suspended, and their leaders, including Ben Kiwanuka were jailed in Luzira Prison. These leaders, along with the ministers jailed earlier would all be rescued by Idi Amin in 1971.

After assuming the post of Executive President following the 1967 constitution, Obote began orienting the country towards socialism. His Nakivubo Pronouncements, referred to as The Common Man's Charter, was not well received, particularly in the business community. Among other things, the policy entailed some aspects of confiscating some private properties without compensating the owners. This policy was anathema to the British government which still held sway over the economic affairs of Uganda. Economics aside, Obote was increasingly becoming a thorn in the flesh to the British, regarding their support for the Apartheid regime in South Africa. Among the Commonwealth leaders, especially those from Africa, he was sticking out like a sore finger, much to the annoyance of Edward Heath, the British Prime Minister.

So, in January 1971, as the Commonwealth Heads of Government (CHOGM) gathered for its bi-annual meeting in Singapore, the British were working behind the scenes to ensure that one of the leaders wouldn't return home after the conference. In a speech tinged with irony, Obote had recently announced that, "I am perhaps the only African leader not afraid of a coup". He must have spoken too soon, while the devil was listening. On January 25, 1971, Idi Amin led the Uganda Army in staging a coup that toppled Milton Obote, setting the country's course into uncharted territory.

Obote might have had good reasons for underestimating Amin based on lack of education, but his charisma was not in doubt. Born in the small village of Koboko, in West Nile District around 1925, he had not had the benefit of attending formal education, as his father abandoned the family when Amin was a young boy. In 1946, he joined the King's African Rifles (KAR) as an assistant cook. His wit and charm caught the eyes of his bosses, who recruited him into the rank and file. There, he distinguished himself through his ferociousness and interrogation technique. He was quickly promoted to the highest possible rank of sergeant afforded to an African soldier at that time, and then between 1952 and 1956, he was dispatched to Kenya, to help quell the Mau Mau insurgency. Amin was also a light heavyweight champion boxer and swimmer between 1951 and 1960.

That day on January 25, 1971, when Amin stepped forward to address the nation as the new leader, most people (including this author), doubted that the voice we heard struggling to read a mere paragraph, would even last a few days in that position. But Amin would prove everyone wrong, and later turn the country into the infamous killing fields with his Kakwa tribesmen. During Amin's first year in office, the country was perhaps at its most relaxed. The Baganda, who had singularly been persecuted by Obote's regime, laid a red carpet for Amin, staging dances everywhere he went, something that appealed to his flamboyant style. Amin returned the favor by releasing all political prisoners, including Ben Kiwanuka. But the grandest act of all, was the return of Kabaka Mutesa's body from London, to give him a royal send off at Kasubi Royal Tombs.

Resistance to Amin's rule began almost immediately, especially from Obote's proteges, some of whom had followed him into exile in Dar-es-Salaam, Tanzania. On September 17, 1972, an armed group of exiles living in Tanzania, invaded Uganda from the border post of Mutukura. Amin's intelligence seemed to have gotten wind of their impending invasion and laid in ambush. The exercise was aborted after the invaders suffered many casualties.

Amidst this stiff resistance, Amin had been consumed with the issue of Asian control of the Ugandan economy. Obote, too, had zeroed on it in his Common Man's manifesto, but Amin had kicked him out of office before he had a chance to take any action. Asians formed the backbone of the commercial sector, controlling perhaps, 75% of it. There were somewhere close to 70,000-75,000 of them, forming less than 1% of the country's population of 10,000,000 at the time, of whom only about 30,000 held Ugandan citizenship. The rest held either British, Indian or Pakistan nationalities, despite having roots in Uganda for generations. Most of the citizens were descendants of the Indian coolies brought in by the British colonialists between 1895-1905, to help in constructing the Kenya-Uganda Railway. Of the total 36,811 coolies who signed contracts to work on the railway, only about 6,700 had stayed behind after the project's completion. But with time, these families multiplied many times over, and were further swelled by the migrations of relatives. The insular nature of Indian communities ensured that they kept control of the commercial sector, much to the detriment of the indigenous Ugandans who wanted to break in. To many leaders, this would be unconscionable.

Then in August 1972, Amin woke up and declared that, in his dream the previous night, Allah (God), had told him to expel the non-citizen Indians "who were milking the economy". It was not an issue discussed in a cabinet meeting, or some council of elders. He gave them 90 days to comply or be removed forcefully. Amin ignored any rational advice given, even where experts pointed out the potential disastrous effects on the economy. Panicky Indian families sold businesses they had built over generations on a dime. Those who couldn't find sellers simply abandoned them or left them in the hands of trusted African assistants. Chaos ensued, as Amin's semi-illiterate soldiers trounced on each other allocating the most attractive businesses among themselves.

At first, prices went down dramatically, as the new owners didn't know how to price anything, sometimes using the collar size of a shirt as the price. Soon, however, the stocks run out, and the new merchants had no clue where to order new stock for replenishment. What were once fancy clothing stores began selling edible consumables such as bananas and chapatis. This phase was followed by galloping inflation that brought the country to its knees. Amin's reaction was to blame the traders. Prominent people started disappearing without a trace.

Among the most prominent disappearances that year were Chief Justice Benedicto Kiwanuka and Frank Kalimuzo, the Vice Chancellor of Makerere University. Upon his release from Luzira prison a year earlier, Ben Kiwanuka, the country's first Prime Minister, had been appointed Chief Justice by Idi Amin. But as Amin's erratic rule went roughshod with the law, Kiwanuka gave advice that was continually ignored. This frustrated the law-and-order Barrister, putting a distance between him and Amin. Some school of thought even suggested that it was his refusal to put his imprimatur on the expulsion of Indians from the country that cost him his own life. He was abducted from his Chambers at the High Court by Amin's soldiers on September 21, 1972. Both men disappeared without a trace.

Following the Yom Kippur War of October 1973, between Israel and the Arab countries, mainly Egypt and Libya, Amin, a Moslem, took advice from the Arab world to close the Israeli Embassy, and expel Israelis from Uganda. Israeli bonds with Uganda go back to the time before the creation of modern Israel, when the British governor of Uganda proposed designating a slice of Uganda as the Jewish homeland. Above all, Israel values Uganda for its own strategic reasons since the Source of the River Nile is located at Jinja on Lake Victoria. It's often said that whoever controls the Nile, controls Egypt. The closure of the Israeli embassy was followed by voluntary closures of western embassies including the US and British, plunging Uganda into diplomatic isolation. The Organization of African Unity (OAU) Summit, which was held in Kampala from July 18 to August 1, 1975, gave Amin some reprieve as he basked in the limelight, including voting him as Chairman for the next year until the next summit. But his glory would be overtaken by events before his term was over. At the end of June 1976, Militants belonging to the Palestine Liberation Organization (PLO), seized a French jetliner en route from Tel-Aviv to Paris, after stopping in Athens, Greece for refueling. They forced the captain to fly to Tripoli, Libya, where a woman, faking pregnancy labor pains was allowed to disembark. After failing to obtain permission to hold the plane in Libya, they sought, and obtained this from Idi Amin, presumably on humanitarian grounds.

However, once on the ground at Entebbe International Airport, it soon dawned on those concerned, especially Israel, that there was collaboration between the PLO and the Baader-Meinhof Gang, also known as the Red Army. Given Israel's experience with terrorism, a decision was made there and then, to rescue the hostages, most of whom were either Israeli citizens, or Jewish. Other nationalities had been released at Entebbe. During the course of the week, Israel engaged Amin in negotiations for release of its nationals as Mossad and the Israeli Defense Forces (IDF) gathered intelligence to plan a course of action. A window of opportunity opened when they learned that Amin would be travelling to Mauritius to handover the chairmanship of the OAU to President Sir Seewoosagur Ramgoolam.

On July 4, 1976, in one of the most daring rescue Missions ever undertaken by any country, IDF commandos descended on Entebbe Airport in a night-time raid dubbed Operation Thunderbolt. After eliminating all the armed terrorists, the 102 hostages were led to the safety of C-130 transporters that had been kept at the ready on the runway. The operation itself suffered only one casualty, Yonatan (Yoni) Netanyahu, elder brother to the previous Israeli Prime Minister, Benjamin Netanyahu. He was the commander of the operation. Among the hostages, one was shot after failing to obey orders instructing all hostages to lie down until told otherwise. The other was Dora Bloch, an old grandmother of dual British/Israeli citizenship, who had been rushed to Mulago Hospital after choking on a fish bone. She was plucked out of the hospital in the dead of the night on Amin's orders following the raid. Her body was only recovered in a Sugar plantation in Lugazi, east of Kampala by Tanzanian soldiers during the putsch that overthrew Amin in 1979. Her remains were returned to her family and buried in Israel. Uganda's casualty list included 50 soldiers, along with several Russian Mig fighters, and major destruction on the airport infrastructure.

From there on, Amin went rogue after the humiliating rescue by Israel. He became more erratic and unpredictable, sometimes conjuring enemies where there were none. On February 17,1977, he earned worldwide condemnation after Anglican Archbishop of Church of Uganda, Janani Luwum, together with two cabinet ministers, Erenayo Oryema, and Charles Oboth Ofumbi, were murdered, and their bodies dumped in a staged car accident. His luck ran out in April 1979 when he provoked his fiercest nemesis in the region, President Julius Nyerere of Tanzania, by claiming a tiny strip of territory on the Tanzanian side of River Kagera, known as the Kagera salient, which lies at the common border with Uganda. In a blitzkrieg, Nyerere sent several battalions of the Tanzanian People's Defense Forces across the border, which gathered more momentum as they were joined by hundreds of Amin's deserting soldiers. In a hurried retreat, Amin fled into exile to Libya, staying for a short time before finally settling in Jeddah Saudi Arabia, where he died on August 16, 2003, after a long stay of 24 years.

Amin's regime had crippled Uganda both economically and socially, leaving a society devoid of any kind of leadership trust. The random killing of innocent citizens during his 8-year rule, had left thousands of children destitute without fathers, and wives deprived of their husbands. The entire social fabric had broken down, leaving a society aching for a Moses to deliver the people out of this chaotic bondage. During the final moments of Amin's impending fall, many opposition groups gathered in the northern Tanzanian city of Moshi to listen, exchange, and promote their own ideologies on how Uganda should be governed following Amin's ouster. Among the competing groups were the country's oldest parties DP and UPC, together with a smattering of old and new lesser-known parties such as the Conservative Party (CP) and the Uganda Patriotic Movement (UPM). President Julius Nyerere who had fervently opposed Amin's rule, was in favor of returning his old pal, Obote to power, arguing that the presidency was still Obote's since it was him who had been illegitimately removed.

However, there were strong counterarguments, such as UPM's allegation that Obote was part of the problem that created Amin, and therefore cannot be the cure for his transgressions. In the end, the Uganda National Liberation Front (UNLF), and its de facto parliament, the National Consultative Council (NCC), settled on a less controversial character by the name of Professor Yusuf Lule, a former Principal of Makerere University College. Lule's low-key style was considered his forte, around which the wounded nation could rally. But this was soon challenged by more militant types such as Yoweri Museveni of UPM, and former Obote Army Chief of Staff and protégé, David Oyite Ojok. They, inter alia, perceived Lule as a conservative who would bend-over backwards to accommodate Buganda's demands for a special status as a federal entity. The critics' fears were not baseless, considering that Lule had been sworn in as interim president in the Luganda language, with Baganda singing "Ekitiibwa kya Buganda", the Buganda Anthem. But, by far, the gravest mistake he committed was attributing the murders and abductions that were ravaging the country at the time, to the Uganda National Liberation Army. President Lule was forcefully removed by the NCC on June 20, 1979, after a 68-day stint in power following a dispute over presidential powers.

In a move that on the outside, appeared to be an appeasement to Buganda, the NCC picked Godfrey Binaisa, a fellow Muganda, to replace Professor Lule as the next president. But Binaisa, a London-trained Barrister with a sharp wit and a wicked sense of humor, was by no means a true friend of Buganda. As Milton Obote's Attorney General during the Buganda Crisis of 1966, Binaisa was the legal mind behind the Republican constitution, dubbed the "pigeonhole constitution", which abolished kingdoms in Uganda, including the 900-year Buganda Kingdom. In an address following his installation as president, he implored the crowd to "Be Nicer" to him, words that rhymed with his name. However, these pleas mostly fell on deaf ears, as competing elements unleashed after Amin's destabilization of the country could not be controlled with a mere wave of the hand. For instance, militarism was on the rise, promoted as the only viable option to control the chaos raging in the country at the time. To curb the rise of militarism in his cabinet, Binaisa relieved Yoweri Museveni of the position of deputy head of the Military Council and assigned him the position of Minister of Regional Cooperation. Oyite Ojok, the other protagonist, was appointed Ambassador to Egypt. Both refused to budge, and instead started on a scheme to dethrone Binaisa himself. He managed to do a little better than his predecessor, lasting 11 months on the job.

The country's slide into turmoil did not stop when the head of the Military Council, Paul Muwanga announced preparations for the 1980 elections. Muwanga was one of a few staunch supporters of exiled President Obote, who was thought to be warming the seat, pending his boss's return. It certainly felt that way, when during the national elections of December 1980, Muwanga hijacked the whole electoral tabulation process after it became apparent that UPC was not doing very well. By the time the results were released about 48 hours later, UPC was declared the winner, including some of the candidates who had conceded defeat prior to Muwanga's announcement. Obote was invited back to reclaim his vacated seat as president. Uganda had entered Joseph Stalin's uncharted territory of "It doesn't matter who votes, it matters more who does the counting". This ill-conceived approach still haunts Uganda's elections more than four decades later.

Although most of the country was shocked and awed by the blatant rigging of the elections, aggrieved parties such as DP were prepared to accept the status quo and move on as the opposition in parliament. However, some of the participants at the Moshi conference vowed to oppose such machinations, even if it meant removing Obote militarily. Yoweri Museveni formed the Popular Resistance Army (PRA), which later merged with Yusuf Lule's Uganda Freedom Fighters (UFF), to create the National Resistance Movement (NRM), with its military wing, the NRA. Other groups contemplating guerilla wars to topple Obote, included Dr. Andrew Kayira's Uganda Freedom Movement (UFM), and Gen. Moses Ali's West Nile Rescue Front. Of all the groups, Museveni's NRA was rated with the highest chance to succeed, based on his previous experience with the Frelimo guerilla warfare in Mozambique. By successfully wooing Muamar Qaddafi to fund the NRA, Museveni solved the biggest obstacle that hamstrings most guerilla movements.

On February 6, 1981, Museveni's comrade-in-arms, the late General Elly Tumwine (died August 25, 2022) fired the NRA's first salvo by attacking the military barracks at Kabamba, belonging to the Uganda Army, then known as the Uganda National Liberation Army (UNLA). This was the beginning of a long and bloody protracted guerilla war that plunged the nation into a black hole of uncertainty. The war would also test Obote's skills as a statesman capable of rallying and unifying the country, instead of being consumed with petty issues of settling old scores. Having no military background of his own, Obote outsourced that role to his top military leaders, giving them carte blanche to pursue the guerilla war with gusto. One of these men was Major-Gen David Oyite Ojok, the UNLA's chief of staff, hailing from Lango District like Obote. He knew Yoweri Museveni well. The two were natural antagonists with differing views of the world. Therefore, the battle between Museveni's NRA and the UNLA led by Oyite Ojok, became one of wills. With the scars left behind by the Amin regime still raw, the country was wary of what many perceived to be an unnecessary war. The war also highlighted another perspective, which seemed to split the country in the middle, into a north-south divide. Museveni's commanders and fighters had been drawn mainly from the west and central (Buganda) regions of the country, while the Uganda Army had been dominated by people from the northern and eastern regions of the country. As the conflict dragged on, many atrocities were committed by both sides as each force was determined to tarnish the other's image. The Luwero Triangle, once an economically vibrant region that produced most of Kampala's food, and Buganda's coffee, became littered with dead bodies and land mines that maimed innocent farmers as they went about their daily chores. After Oyite Ojok was killed in a suspicious helicopter crash on December 2, 1983, Museveni's side appeared to gain strength, but the enthusiasm tapered soon after, ushering in a stalemate period which would last for another three years of death and destruction.

On July 29, 1985, a group of senior Acholi soldiers in the UNLA, angered by Obote's promotion of fellow Langi tribesman Opon Acak to chief of staff, over more experienced Acholi veterans, staged a bloodless coup that deposed Milton Obote from the presidency for the second time. Obote's replacement was a low-key aging Acholi military General named Tito Okello Lutwa. The NRA seized on this opportunity of internal ethnic fighting to escalate their operations and gain an upper hand. In a last-ditch effort, the Okello regime invited the NRA to join them in a government of national unity. Museveni half-heartedly led his top lieutenants to the Peace Talks (dubbed peace jokes), presided over by then Kenyan President Daniel Arap Moi in Nairobi. But while the talks went on, Museveni's fighters kept their eyes on prize. By the time the parties returned to Kampala in early January, it was apparent that Okello's government had no room left to maneuver. On January 26, 1986, Museveni's NRA captured Kampala, installed him as president, promising a new fundamental change from past regimes.

Yoweri Museveni was born in Kajara County (Ntungamo District) to Amos Kaguta and Esteri Kokundeka, on August 15, 1944. He attended Kyamate Primary School, where he met his lifelong friend, the late Eriya Kategaya, with whom they would later cofound the Front for National Salvation (FRONASA). He proceeded to Mbarara High School, and then on to Ntare School before enrolling at the University of Dar-es-Salaam in 1967, where he obtained a bachelor's degree in political science and economics in 1970. Museveni's political activism started germinating at Ntare School in the mid-1960's, and blossomed at Dar, from where he linked up with the Frelimo Movement in Mozambique, led by the late President Samora Machel. His activism was already apparent in 1971, when he could be heard denouncing President Idi Amin on Radio Tanzania. By the time he led his rag-tag guerilla army to power in Uganda, Museveni was already a well-known entity, albeit only a mythical one since most people had never seen him.

From the get set, Museveni showed a strong disinclination to share the limelight with anyone else. He is the kind of leader who quickly takes personal credit for anything good that happens in the country, but will equally as fast, assign blame to someone else when things don't go his way. In almost all events that have shaped the course of Uganda in the last 36 years, the buck has stopped with him. At first, this was viewed as a strength, as the nation teetering on the brink of disaster, needed a decisionmaker with a steady hand. However, as time went by, the nation began to realize that individual decisions without a collegial approach were, more often detrimental to the country's overall interest goals. Museveni's approach has been to completely dominate and overwhelm every tenet of opposition, that many capable people have ended up being scared out of even contemplating trying, for fear of being humiliated.

The majority in the cohort that started the NRM with him, or even those who participated in the bush war in Luwero, have since abandoned him after he relentlessly frustrated their ambitions. In September 2022, the last of about 30 senior military officers that started the Bush War were retired. Some, like his former personal physician, Dr. Kiiza Besigye, or his longest serving army commander, Maj-Gen Mugisha Muntu, have gone on to start and head their own parties. Their success has, however, been hampered by the continuous onslaught by Museveni forces, bent on inflicting both mental and sometimes physical torture, to prevent them from gaining any advantage over him. In this regard, he used his own appointed attack dogs, such as former Inspector General of Police, Gen. Kale Kayihura, a trusted lieutenant, and one-time aide-de-camp, to inflict maximum damage on his opponents. In 2011, following protests over a fraudulent election, Gen. Kayihura's police arrested Mr. Museveni's main opponent, and former personal physician, Dr. Kiiza Besigye. In the ensuing scuffle, one security officer named Arineitwe Bwana, broke Besigye's car window, hammered him with gun butts, while pepper-spraying his eyes until he was almost blind. The police further denied him access to immediate medical attention, leaving him agonizing in pain. The incident was captured live and played to a worldwide audience on You-Tube. It took the intervention of some western ambassadors, including that of the US, Britain, and Germany, to intervene and send the opposition leader to Nairobi, where he spent nearly a month recovering. In connection with these atrocities, on September 13, 2019, General Kayihura and his family were barred from entering, or conducting business in the United States, due to the human rights violations instigated while he was at the helm. Human rights organizations such as Amnesty International had long forwarded his name to the International Criminal Court (ICC) for prosecution. But those who thought the removal of Gen. Kayihura would end police and army brutality in Uganda were in for a surprise when it returned with a vengeance in late October 2019. Following a student strike protesting a recent move by the University authorities to increase tuition by 15%, military police descended on the campus of Uganda's oldest University, arresting, clobbering, and some say, raping a few of the female students caught up in the riot. Although the Vice Chancellor, along with top officials of the Ministry of Education have called these stories exaggerated, the damage to one of Africa's prestigious centers of learning cannot be underestimated. It should also be noted that the nation's current Minister of Education is Janet Kataha Museveni, wife of Uganda's long-serving President Yoweri Museveni. This incident was not alone in isolation. On Monday, November 4, riot police intercepted opposition leader Dr. Kiiza Besigye's motorcade, headed for Nambole Stadium, where he was slated to address a rally. After disobeying orders to disembark from his car, police directed a high-powered water hose at him, which almost ejected him from the vehicle, save for his driver and other people inside, who held his legs very firmly. This was followed by a senior police Superintendent named Rashid Agero, smashing the vehicle's windshield with a gun butt, and pepper-spraying the opposition leader in the face. These actions, conducted in broad daylight in front of cameras, have gone viral on social media, and received worldwide condemnation. Opposition leaders are currently putting together a petition, in which they seek up to a million or more signatures, which they will then present to the ICC requesting action against the perpetrators of these heinous crimes in Uganda. Like President Trump of the US, Museveni can be charming to his cheerleaders, but turn incendiary towards the same people once they stop clapping. He also never apologizes to those he transgresses, believing that would be a sign of weakness.

That's what he did to his now deceased childhood friend, Eriya Kategaya. In 2005, when the veteran politician opposed the president on changing the constitution to remove the article regarding presidential term limits, Mr. Museveni dropped him from his cabinet, along with other like-minded but formerly close advisors like Jaberi Bidandi-Ssali and Miria Matembe. He used the same tactics in 2016, to frustrate and crush the campaign of Patrick Amama Mbabazi, his longtime protégé and smooth operating secretary of the ruling party, NRM. For a long time, Ugandans had been duped by Mr. Museveni into believing that Mbabazi was his preferred heir apparent. This lie was peppered by heaping all kinds of titles on him, at one time holding as many as three portfolios simultaneously, including Prime Minister, Defense Minister, and Secretary General of the NRM, earning him the moniker "super minister". But all this fizzled away in 2015, when Mr. Mbabazi, perhaps tired of playing second fiddle, declared that he was challenging his boss for the nomination of the party's presidency, and as flag-bearer for the top job in the country. Suddenly, the gloves were off, and he was no longer the blue-blooded indefatigable close confidant of the president. First, he was relieved of the premiership, and secretary generalship of the party. His wife was also dropped from chairing the women's wing of the party. Then his campaign was hounded by the police and other state organs at every turn, including those from the security ministry he once headed, causing him to perform miserably in the general election. Then, when he filed a petition case of election-related fraudulent activities against the incumbent at the Superior Court, his lawyer's office was broken into by, (you guessed it, security operatives), the night before the court's hearing, all evidence taken away and destroyed. His lawyer nearly choked as he tried to answer the Chief Justice's near comical question of "Where is your client's evidence?".

The three branches of government have been so dominated by the Executive branch, that the Legislative (parliament), and the Judiciary, have only been reduced to rubber-stamping the president's position. The president has, for instance, authorized the police and the UPDF (army), to intervene in parliamentary proceedings by physically ejecting members who were protesting the Age Limit bill which directly affected the president. The judiciary also witnessed such incidents, when a pseudo group known as the Black Mambas, stormed the High Court and re-arrested some opposition members who had just been granted bail by the judge. One former senior judge referred to that incident as "the rape of the Temple of Justice". In one unforgettable remark, the president said that "the judges' role is to adjudicate over chicken and goat thefts, but not to determine the course and direction of the nation". He recently stated that most of judiciary's court rulings, especially those in connection with land, will be ignored by the executive branch, because, according to him, they are not "pro-people".

The 1995 Constitution which took a painstaking five years to draft and promulgate, has since undergone two major shakeups. The first was to remove the article on term limits and allow the president to run indefinitely, and the more recent one in 2018, expunged the age limits, also to benefit the same individual who would have been beyond the original stipulated age limit of 75 years at the last presidential election held in January 2021. The continual moving of goal posts to suit the megalomaniac egos of one individual has left the country despondent and devoid of good leadership to elevate it to the next level. While all this culpability may be pointed towards the president, we cannot exonerate the enablers, mainly the retinue of NRM cadres, praise-singers, and cheerleaders, driven by cupidity, and whose livelihood depends on the longevity of the Dear Leader whom they continue to hold hostage. In a January 5, 2020 Sunday Monitor article, Labor State Minister Mwesigwa Rukutana referred to Mr. Museveni as a "super human, given to Uganda by God, citing his intelligence, virility,and agility as special attributes that distinguish the president as a one-of-a-kind species. It takes two to tangle. When the Executive Branch and its titular head usurps power from other organs of government, the whole system suffers. Even worse, when individuals fear to speak out against malfeasance committed against other individuals or groups, simply because they aren't part of those targeted, that marks the beginning of the end for that society. We are reminded of the immortal words uttered by Pastor Martin Niemoller, a prominent Lutheran pastor, used in repudiating Adolph Hitler's Third Reich,

"First, they came for the socialists, and I could not speak out because I was not a socialist. Next, they came for the trade unionists, and I could not speak out because I was not in the trade union. Then they came for the Jews, and I could not speak out because I was not a Jew. And, finally, they came for me, and there was no one left to speak out for me."

To his credit, Museveni inherited a devastated economy, and a country that was engrossed in chaos, and stabilized it into one that experiences normal problems. It took a very long time to arrive at this stage, and naturally, people get impatient. There are many things he could have done differently to achieve better results. A case in point is the way the NRM government handled the internal displacement of people in the northern region. The two-decade war fought against Joseph Kony's Lord's Resistance Army inflicted deep wounds among the people of northern Uganda, including depriving them of opportunities to benefit from a growing economy in the rest of the country. The result has been the creation of a permanent underclass due to an income gap between north and south, which will need Solomonic efforts to bridge. The president also continues to take a cavalier attitude towards corruption which has eaten away and destroyed the social and financial fabric of the nation. The country continues to lack capacity to undertake basic projects such as construction of basic roads and bridges that would elevate it to the next level. For the longest period during Museveni's rule, the growth of the economy has been sustained by "a global good will", of not wishing to see the whole Great Lakes region disintegrate like the DRC and South Sudan and memories of Rwanda's genocide.

An old wise Chinese saying goes like this: "If you wish to travel fast, go alone, but if you wish to go far, travel with friends". The "I alone can fix it" mantra, or the notion that one mortal human being can monopolize all ideas, as to be considered indispensable, is to say the least, silly and a non-starter. We can also follow the wisdom implied in the book "Tous Les Hommes Sont Mortels" (All men are mortal) by Simone de Beauvoir. Any society that doesn't embrace the dynamic that change is an essential component of progress, becomes a victim of its own circumstances which relegates it to a path of stagnation. Good leaders are always conscious of their limits and strive to nurture the next generation to pilot the engine of state. Those who fail to internalize this age-old wisdom, like Julius Caesar, soon get gobbled up by the young and restless. Mr. Museveni's meaningful contribution days are behind him. After 36 years at the helm, he and his courtiers can no longer blame the ills of the country on "past leaders" that more than half of the population never saw. The median age of Uganda's population is only 15.9 years, implying that half of the population has been born during his rule. For a man who once diagnosed Africa's problem as stemming from leaders who perpetuate themselves in power, it appears the old man with a bowler hat owes his country an explanation and an apology regarding his longevity in State House. As of 2022, Uganda remains in the unenviable position of never having transferred power democratically and peacefully from one leader to another in its 60 years since independence on October 9, 1962.

To many, he has now become the symbol of those past leaders he excoriated. It's abundantly clear to any casual observer, that his perpetual contests for the presidency are no longer based on the wishes of the people. Without using state security organs to coerce his opponents and beat the ruled into submission, he would have long retreated to his country home of Rwakitura, to pursue cattle-keeping, a vocation he professes to love more than politics. Over the past 20 years, each time he's faced a real challenge over his rule, he retreats into incoherent verbosity that degenerates into totally irrelevant history. To him, the history of the country begins with his ascendency into power in 1986, and he seems to believe the country will stop functioning once he is gone. He has regurgitated the same platitudes that have not yielded many results in the past, leading one to wonder, if this isn't the kind of insanity defined by Albert Einstein, as doing the same thing over, and over again, but expecting different outcomes. Strong leaders listen more and talk less. All the efforts he invested in liberation movements and fighting to rid the country of megalomaniacs like Idi Amin, will be meaningless if in the end, he can't create a free and progressive society. By his own intransigence, he becomes a clear and present danger. His efforts to sustain himself in power place the nation ever closer to the precipice of a chaotic end akin to that of Idi Amin.

In 2015, one of Mr Museveni's bush generals who headed the government's intelligence services spilled the beans on a long-held open secret. He issued a veiled message, that there was a "Muhoozi Project", a reference to Museveni's son who was on a fast-track promotion in the Uganda People's Defense Forces, (UPDF), to make him eligible as an heir-apparent to succeed his father as president. The President dismissed that as idle talk, although the promotions continued to be heaped on the son. The son, who was a Lt-Col at that time embarked on twitting relentlessly, to make his presence felt, oftentimes violating the UPDF code of conduct that prevents serving military personnel from engaging in politics. Any other military officer that has gone afoul of this rule has been reprimanded and scolded by Mr Museveni, but not his son. Muhoozi's twitter storm has even caused some diplomatic brouhaha, like the time he posted a message suggesting that Uganda supports the Tigrayan rebels over the Ethiopian Federal army. The president had to dispatch the foreign minister, with Muhoozi himself, to cool things down. However, the spoiled brat outdid himself at the beginning of October 2022, when the then senior military officer, and Commander of the UPDF land forces, twitted that his forces could capture Nairobi, the Kenyan capital in less than two weeks. It's not very clear what provoked the first son, who has been friendly with outgoing President Uhuru Kenyatta.

Nevertheless, the twit generated a mega diplomatic firestorm, forcing his father, the president, to personally issue an immediate apology to both Kenyans and Ugandans. But what followed remains even more puzzling. Mr Museveni elevated his son from the rank of Lt-General to full General, although he relieved him of the land forces command. That promotion means there are three 4-Star generals in the Museveni family, including himself, and his younger brother Salim Saleh. After the latest imbroglio with his son, there are all indications that the man who once told the nation, that the main problem with Africa, are leaders who perpetuate themselves in power, will seek yet another term in 2026. He will be 82 at that time. The Luganda language, the most widely spoken in Uganda, has a rich vocabulary. The word "kupalappalanya" refers to someone adept at finding unconvincing excuses to justify his failures. In that regard, Mr. Museveni can be described as a 'Master of kupalappalanya", when it comes to his ever-changing stories of why he has not delivered a Singapore-like economy that he promised nearly forty years ago when he shot his way to State House. Every independence-day speech is delivered with a new blame on why his NRM regime could not meet its goals. If it's not his predecessors, whom he sometimes derides as swine, it will be the "ignorant opposition in parliament", or lately, "those arrogant former colonialists in London and Brussels". The one thing you'll never hear him talk about, is his cronyism, that has rendered most institutions in the country dysfunctional.

Back in my university student days, a group of young men wanted the Dean of students to extend female visiting hours beyond the 2.00-7.00 pm slot by another two hours to 9.00 pm. The Dean listened attentively, after which, upon finishing their presentation, he turned to them and gave them a piece of fatherly advice, "Young men, take it from me, what you couldn't do in all that time you already have, you may not do even if I gave you the whole night". Mr. Museveni, too, could draw wisdom from the Dean's advice.

"L'etat c'est moi", apres moi, c'est le deluge or, literally speaking, "I am the state", after me, it's a flood, is a phrase often attributed to King

Louis XIV who ruled France for 72 years, from 1643 to 1715, in a reign known as "absolutism", due to the heavy-handedness of the monarchy.

Also referred to as "Le Roi Soleil", or the Sun King, Louis XIV transformed France like no other monarch before him. His belief in his Divine right to be king, combined with the longevity of his reign, helped him transform France from a medieval kingdom, to one of the most admired countries in the world.

Like M7, the king strongly believed in a centralized state, ruled from the center. By building his magnificent palace at Versailles and compelling many members of the nobility to reside there, he managed to pacify the aristocracy, many of whose members had participated in the Fronde rebellion.

The French monarch sought to eliminate the remnants of feudalism, which further helped him consolidate his position as an absolute monarch, a position not quite unlike President M7's neutralization of the Kabaka, and the other kings, with his declaration of himself as the "Ssabagabe", or King of Kings.

As the leading European power during his reign, France was involved in three major wars, with its neighbors, namely, the Franco-Dutch War, the war of the League of Augsburg, and the War of the Spanish Succession. Like Louis XIV, M7"s war-mongering efforts in the Great Lakes Region area are unsurpassed, having been instrumental in the 1979 Uganda-Tanzania Liberation War, the 1981-86 Luwero Triangle War, the 1990-94 Rwanda Liberation War, the Congolese war against Mobutu in the late 1990s, the Somali war against Al Shabab, and more recently, his adventurism to prop up the shaky regime in Juba, South Sudan.

Uganda's GDP continued to enjoy steady growth but has slowed from the galloping 7% pace it enjoyed in the 1990's and early 2000's. It should, however, be emphasized that all the buoyancy in the economy started from a very low base following the turmoil in the 1970's and 80's. The five years up to 2016 averaged a growth rate of 4.5% according to the World Bank Group. Covid-19's lockdown drastically affected the country's growth trajectory, with GDP barely growing. Any slowdown affects the country's ability to increase income and reduce poverty. The earlier slowdown was attributed to instability in South Sudan, a main agricultural export destination, and drought conditions which impacted agriculture negatively. Most of the country's agricultural production is rain-fed, creating a downside risk to farmers' incomes and tax revenue collections. The forecast for good performance in 2019 assumed prevalence of good weather, and increased FDI flows as the country prepares to start building the oil pipeline, possibly in 2022.

The Uganda-Tanzania Oil Pipeline (EACOP) is running into headwinds with the bureaucrats in Brussels over environmental issues. President M7 is up in arms against anything that may interfere with "my oil", as he sometimes refers to that national resource. But the French giant oil company Total Energies SE, which is underwriting the funding for the construction cannot afford to operate outside the laws set within the European Union. The company group Chairman, Mr.Patrick Pouyanne, is currently butting heads with the EU Parliament's resolution to slow down the pipeline construction over environmental and human rights issues. M7, who has called the Brussels officials arrogant and racist, risks suffering from the wrath they could apply to a non-compliant EU company.

The fiscal deficit widened to 4.7% of GDP in 2018 because of continued borrowing for infrastructure, mostly funded by Chinese loans. The nation's total public debt stock amounted to US$10.5 billion at the end of March 2018, of which US$7.2 billion was foreign, while US$3.3 billion was domestic. The debt-to-GDP ratio stood at 40.0%, of which 28.1% was external. Although the country's debt has jumped significantly in the last ten years, it is still considered to be at a low risk of distress. Headline inflation was at 3.2% per annum. Despite heavy investment in infrastructure, electric power, water, sanitation, and health facilities remain inadequate to support a growing economy. Another downside risk is the country's fast-growing population, currently estimated at close to 40 million, growing at 3.0% per annum. This is one of the fastest rates in the world, and poses a challenge to policy makers, as it whittles resources away faster than they can be replenished.

Ugandans went gung-ho when Tullow Oil Company of the UK,

proved what had been an open secret since the 1930's, that Uganda had deposits of crude oil. The 2006 announcement put the estimated reserves at 6.5 billion barrels, of which about 1.4 billion are recoverable. However, the nation's amplified wealth expectations have had to be tamed as each year comes and goes with no sign of oil coming out of the ground. The current scheduled beginning of pumping and export is anticipated within the next two years, but lack of supporting infrastructure such as the Masindi-Tanga pipeline whose construction has yet to be started, may again delay implementation. The scheduled production suffered another setback which is sure to cause further delay. Tullow Oil Company, one of the pioneers in Uganda's oil search, failed to sell a 21.5% stake, worth US$900 million to Total E&P in August 2019. As a result, Total E&P, the French Oil giant which is in a triangular partnership with Chinese oil company CNOOC and Tullow, suspended operations indefinitely. The dispute appears to be over the taxes Tullow would incur over the sale, and the costs the partners would inherit.

There are also other factors at play, such as an anticipated global recession, which would curtail consumption of oil products. If this happens, the first casualties would be oil projects in the pipeline such as Uganda's with high initial development costs. Uganda's oil is waxy, requiring the entire 1,400-kilometer pipeline to be heated to allow for a smooth flow. Although President Museveni recently assured the nation that production is on schedule, there are jitters within the Ministry of Finance and Bank of Uganda, that the country may not generate the income necessary soon enough, to service the nation's debt, now above 50% of GDP. The nation's energy sector has improved considerably in the past ten years, especially with increased electric generation. Two major hydro-electric dams, Karuma (600 MW), soon to be commissioned and Isimba (183 MW), commissioned in March 2019, along with solar projects, will add nearly 1,000 MW to the national grid. The country's target was to raise total capacity generation to 3,500 MW by end of 2019, but poor design of the dams at both Isimba and Karuma, that has left gaping cracks in the structures may trim this power generation to lower levels.

Uganda should take every precaution to avoid the "oil curse" that has afflicted countries such as Venezuela, Nigeria, Gabon, Angola, and Equatorial Guinea, where the development of the oil sector was at the expense of other sectors and ushered in uncontrollable corruption. The Governor of the Central Bank recently warned that the accelerated public borrowing predicated on future oil revenues, may be a precursor to the dreaded resource curse. Uganda's nascent oil sector already has all the right ingredients and boilerplates of an oil curse. With a quasi-military government headed by a control-freak whose extended family already controls a disproportionate chunk of the economy, it would be foolhardy for the gullible citizens to imagine the thoroughbreds of Kiruhura would maintain a hands-off policy from the goose that lays the golden eggs. Ask that fly on the wall inside State House, what the old man with a bowler hat talks about with the potentate of Equatorial Guinea, whose son Teodorin purchased a US$36 million mansion in Malibu, a suburb of Los Angeles, California, and was the silent bidder who bought the King of Soul, Michael Jackson's jewel-bedecked glove, all that on an Agriculture minister's salary of $60,000 a year! Despite the linguistic, cultural and age differences, the two long-term dictators have struck a curiously close relationship that has seen President Teodoro Mbasogo Obiang visit his pal in Uganda several times in the recent past. During the most recent visit in October 2019, as the chief guest at Uganda's independence celebrations, the two were seen visiting a refugee camp in Kiryandongo, District, a stone throw close to Uganda's main Oil drilling site. But anyone thinking the megalomaniac of Malabo's visit to the refugee camp, was driven by philanthropy, is unaware that Equatorial Guinea has one of the highest malnutrition rates in the world, despite registering the highest income per capita on the continent. The discovery of oil, or black gold as it's often referred to, is not always a blessing, especially for poor countries hoping to live off its bounty. If its management is in the wrong hands, the sudden windfall can spinoff all sorts of unintended consequences. The large inflows of cash tend to be concentrated in a few hands, usually the leader's family and the minions who surround him. This creates tension between those with access and the ones left out, leading to violence. Besides the monetary side, there are other negative issues such as pollution of water tables and major spills such as the Exxon-Valdes in Alaska, or the Deepwater Horizon gush in the Macondo Prospect operated by BP, which dumped over 1 million gallons of crude into the Gulf of Mexico beginning April 20, 2010. The late Sheikh Zaki Yamani, (died February 23, 2021), the long serving Saudi Oil Minister, and one of the founders of OPEC, once remarked that he wished Saudi Arabia had discovered that much water instead of oil, while his counterpart in Venezuela referred to oil as the excrement of the devil.

The country has a regional comparative advantage in agriculture, endowed with a unique supply of water resources that it can put to better use for commercial agriculture. At 12,000,000 metric tons per annum, Uganda only trails India as # 2 in banana production in the world, although most are domestically consumed. It is also Africa's second largest coffee producer behind Ethiopia, ranking #8 in the world at 288,000 tons annually, again one notch behind India's 348,000 tons. The World Food Program sources most of the corn and beans it needs to feed the starving masses in South Sudan and DRC from Uganda. Besides oil and other minerals such as gold, copper, iron-ore, tin, uranium etc, the country is endowed with tourist resources including the Big Five (Elephants, Buffalo, Rhino. Lion and Leopard). Other tourist attractions include the giant mountain gorillas, (of which there are less than 1,000 left in the world), water rafting on the River Nile, and scaling high mountains such as Mt Rwenzori (Mountains of the Moon), at 16,762 ft, and Mt Elgon (Masaba) at 14,177 ft, and the picturesque sub-montane region of Kisoro, shielded by the towering conical non-active volcanoes of Muhabura, Mugahinga and Sabinyo along the tri-country borders of Uganda, Rwanda and the Democratic Republic of Congo (DRC). More resources should be channeled towards developing modern tourist facilities to cater for numbers beyond the 1.5 million annual visitors to the country.

CHAPTER 17

The Kenya Colony (originally known as East African Colony) was conceived out of gunboat diplomacy between Britain and Germany. On August 6, 1885, a German flotilla of five gunboats sailed into the lagoons of Zanzibar, with their guns at the ready. Their mission, under Chancellor Bismarck of Germany, was to force then Sultan Barghash of Zanzibar, to cede his claims over the vast mainland territory that includes most of present-day Kenya, and part of Tanzania. By then, the British were already eyeing the Kingdom of Buganda deep in the interior, after the widely circulated letter by explorer Henry Morton Stanley, published in the London Daily Telegraph, earlier in 1875. They saw an opportunity to gain territory which would allow them easy access to the sea. The British convinced the Germans to limit their sphere of influence to territory south of Lake Victoria, over what's modern Tanzania today. But after this agreement, the wheeler-dealing Karl Peters told the British that the territory negotiated did not include the Kingdom of Buganda. He hastened to Mengo, the seat of the Kabaka of Buganda, and offered to make Buganda a German protectorate. Meanwhile, a British maverick by the name of Captain

Frederick Lugard, who had arrived at the Kabaka's palace from the coast, to run the territory as head of the Imperial British East African Company, (IBEAC), raised the prospects of war with Germany.

Lugard, a British subject born January 22, 1858, at Fort St. George, Madras, India, of missionary parents, had obtained military training at the Royal Military College, Sandhurst, followed by service in India and stints in Nigeria. His promising military career in India was cut short by a disastrous love affair with a married woman. Undermined by this, he initially sought a life of oblivion by following in the footsteps of famed British explorer Dr. David Livingstone, to chase Arab slave traders and stop slavery in the East African region, even getting seriously wounded near Lake Nyasa (Lake Malawi) in the process. A true bushwhacker, in Buganda, he had quickly imposed order over feuding Baganda chiefs, divided by loyalty towards the newly introduced foreign religions of Protestantism, Catholicism and Islam. He signed a treaty of allegiance with Kabaka Mwanga II, went on to sign treaties with the other regional kings, and was instrumental in securing Uganda as a protectorate for the British. His firm negotiating style, buttressed by a regiment of soldiers with their famous maxim guns nearby, ensured that his final decision weighed heavily on his opponents.

Lugard later returned to Nigeria, to undertake the unification of the Muslim north and Christian and animist south, which he achieved in 1914, against hostilities where he once survived a poisoned arrow shot into his head. He was, at the same time fending off rivalry from the French who were quickly gobbling up and expanding territory in west and central Africa. In a conjured compromise, British Prime Minister Lord Salisbury offered the Germans the tiny island of Heligoland, a deal that was accepted. This deal would, however, later haunt the British as Heligoland served as a German naval base against them in two world wars. The Sultan who was mostly ignored during the negotiations, was allowed retention of a strip of land 10 miles wide from the coast. In a joint British-German boundary commission, a line was drawn from the coast in a northwesterly direction towards Mt Kilimanjaro, and on to Lake Victoria, then another westward at latitude 1 degree south, marking the boundaries between Kenya and Tanganyika. Tanzania was formed as a union between mainland Tanganyika and the off-coastal island of Zanzibar on April 26, 1964.

Now, the British had a vast East African territory extending as far as Equatoria Province of present-day South Sudan. But they were reluctant to fully commit themselves about running their acquisition on account of the cost involved. Instead, they opted to follow the model in Rhodesia, where the swash-buckling Cecil Rhodes' British South African Company would run the territory for profit on behalf of the British Government. So, a commercial company, the Imperial British East African Company (IBEAC) was chartered for the purpose in 1888. Told of the prospects of the British plan to abandon Uganda on account of the cost of running it, Lugard hurriedly took a trip to London to, among other things, plead with the colonial secretary, ensuring that the British stayed on, but also debunk stories about his brutality.

With the Uganda protectorate secured in 1894, and Lugard's ability to run it having been tested by factional fighting, the British chose to terminate IBEAC's charter to run the territory on their behalf, compensating the company with 250,000 British pounds. This action left the larger Kenyan territory wide open, forcing the British to also declare it a protectorate in 1895. The same year, the British decided that the vast territory would need a railway to facilitate transportation of goods and services to serve the hinterland. To raise the revenue for constructing the railway, they encouraged settlement of people of European origin to establish large farms on the most fertile arable land, especially in the Rift Valley and surrounding highlands. Most of these settlers came from South Africa, where rigid racial laws already existed. The colonial government did this by formulating policies that displaced the indigenous populations such as the Maasai, Kikuyu, Kalenjin, and Nandi, relegating them to crowded reservations on less productive land, not unlike what the Boers of South Africa had done to the indigenous population. Vast chunks of ancestral land were given away in this manner, causing a lot of resentment towards the colonial government and the settlers. The settlers, with connivance from the colonial government applied a similar system of exploitative laws, stripping owners of their lands with no recourse to action.

Prominent local leaders like Chief Lenana of the Maasai, were first tricked with mere trinkets and bling-bling, into cooperating with the administration, then later coerced into signing phony agreements whose implications they didn't understand. At the apex of his power, Lenana was courted and feted by the high and mighty of the colonial government, showered with gifts, and praised for his wisdom. They used him to cajole and suppress dissent among other Maasai chiefs who resisted white settlers occupying their traditional grazing lands in Laikipia and other places. He was also co-opted as an ally in assisting the colonialists in fighting and driving the Kikuyu and other tribes from their ancestral lands. But in 1911 when he lay dying of dysentery, a disease they could have cured, no help was forthcoming. Instead, then Governor Girouard Percy showed up to view the emaciated body of the chief and shower him with posthumous praises. He was quick to remind the grieving Maasai, to honor the chief's purportedly wishes, top of which was to leave the Kenya highlands to the white settlers. Chief Lenana had been coxed into signing away his tribal land rights in the 1911 Agreement, known as "the tragedy of the commons". When construction of the railway was started, the British imported many Indentured Indian coolies mainly from the Punjab region of India and present-day Pakistan. Most had already acquired construction experience building railways on the Indian sub-continent. They did not have an entirely smooth ride.

Besides the tropical diseases such as malaria, endemic to the region, they would face the menace of vicious animals such as the notorious "Man-eaters of Tsavo", a pair of mane-less lions that devoured up to135 of the coolies, before being hunted and shot down by Col. John Henry Patterson in 1898. Some of the coolies stayed behind after the railway project was completed in 1901. They brought their families, multiplied, and established themselves in the field of commerce, creating a buffer between the indigenous people and the colonialists. But their cozy relationship with the oppressor didn't endear them to the oppressed. Later, when independence came, and most of the white settlers and administrators left, attention and scrutiny would be focused on this group, which now controlled the economy in the region. In Kenya, a delicate dance took place regarding the issue of economic dominance, but in Uganda, the emergence of Idi Amin turned it into a mega-kiloton explosion that resulted in the mass expulsion of nearly 70,000 Asians from the country beginning September 1972.

The establishment of a legislative council in 1919 which only allowed white settlers to participate, aroused other groups into action. They too, wanted representation over issues that touched their daily lives. As early as 1920, the Indian community turned down an offer of two seats in the council, arguing that these didn't represent their community. In 1921, Harry Thuku formed the Young Kikuyu Association (later known as the East African Association), with the purpose of demanding for the recovery of the appropriated Kikuyu land. Jomo Kenyatta (original name Kamau Ngengi, later baptized Johnstone) joined this group in 1922. When this group was suppressed in 1925, it quickly morphed into another known as the Kikuyu Central Association, primarily with the same objectives.

In 1928, Jomo Kenyatta became the General Secretary and editor of the organization's newspaper known as Mwigithania (The Unifier), sacrificing his Municipal job in the process. The paper's aim was to bring together all Kikuyu factions for a common purpose of opposing European occupation of their land but disguised this by emphasizing self-improvement. Its tone was relatively benign, so the government allowed its publication. However, the tone changed after a British commission recommended close cooperation among the nascent East African colonies of Kenya, Uganda and Tanganyika, which the settlers applauded with a view towards internal self-governance. To the Kikuyu, this would mean entrenchment of the settlers, leading to permanent dispossession of their land. In February 1929, Kenyatta went to London to testify against the committee's recommendations, but the Colonial Secretary wouldn't even meet him. In March 1930, Kenyatta penned an eloquent and elaborate letter in the London Times, in which he spelled out five main grievances that needed the immediate attention of the government. The list constituted, (1) security of land tenure with emphasis on returning to indigenous owners, land allocated to settlers. (2) need for increase in educational facilities, (3) repeal of the hut tax on women, which forced some into prostitution, (4) demand for more African representation in the Council, and (5) non-interference in traditional customs. He further warned the colonial administration about "a potential explosion" and dire consequences if African demands were ignored, referring to this explosion as the one thing any sane human being would wish to avoid. In 1932, Kenyatta testified again at the Carter Land Commission in which it was agreed to compensate a few appropriated areas but wouldn't give in an inch on the white highlands. The Kikuyu would remain relegated to crowded reserves.

Kenyatta proceeded to the Soviet Union and spent two years at Moscow University. He left Moscow and returned to Britain, where he studied anthropology and economics at the London School of Economics, his thesis later published into a book entitled "Facing Mount Kenya" in 1938. It was also at this time, that he changed his name to Jomo (burning spear) Kenyatta. In London, which had become a popular destination for black nationalists, Kenyatta took part in protests launched against the Italian invasion of Ethiopia, as well as helping in organizing the fifth Pan-African Congress held in Manchester in October 1945. The conference was chaired by W.E.B Dubois, pre-eminent US civil rights leader, and was attended by future African independence luminaries such Kwame Nkrumah.

Regarding representation in the Legislative Council, it wasn't until 1944, that the council resorted to tokenism by appointing one African member to represent the majority population. More demands followed, and grudgingly, by 1950, the number had risen to 8, still outnumbered by representatives of much smaller populations of the white settlers and Indians. In September 1946, Kenyatta returned to Kenya and was elected to the presidency of the Kenya African Union, in June 1947. His tenure would, however, be overtaken by events beyond his control, as the explosion he had predicted in the 1930's began to unfold.

Convinced that nothing taken from them would be handed back on a silver platter, a militant wing of the Kenya African Union (KAU) known as the Anake a 40 (aka kiama cha 40) had formed in 1940. The leadership of this group included Mwangi Macharia, Dedan Kimathi, Bildadi Kaggia, Stanley Mathenge, Donatus Mathenge and Waruhiu

Itote. It was this group that morphed itself into what came to be known as the Mau Mau. The members took a vow of secrecy, and their main objective was to make the country ungovernable, leading to the exit of the white settlers. Their first acts of sabotage started in October 1952. The government immediately reacted with a clampdown, including the arrest of the leaders of the KAU, and Jomo Kenyatta. In April 1953, Kenyatta was sentenced to 7 years in prison. However, any attempt by the government to link him to the activities of the Mau Mau gained him more worldwide attention. Moreover, his arrest, rather than stopping the militant group's activities, instead appeared to strengthen their resolve. Dedan Kimathi, who is a celebrated idol in Kenya today, was arrested by the colonial government in 1956, and hanged at Kamiti Maximum Prison on February 18,1957. He was replaced in his leadership role by Bildadi Kaggia, who once told his schoolteacher that, "Kenya needed warriors to send the British back", after she retorted that the days of warriors hunting animals were over. As more demands for independence manifested themselves from all corners of the continent, pressure came to bear on the British government to steer these countries towards majority rule. In 1960, with Kenyatta still under detention, the Kenya African National Union (KANU) party was organized by other nationalists of the day, who included Jaramogi Oginga Odinga and Tom Mboya. The party elected Kenyatta as its president and refused to cooperate with the government until he was released. However, the government continued having misgivings about Kenyatta's role in the Mau Mau, until he held a press conference during which he assuaged them that Europeans and other races would have a place in an independent Kenya, provided they were willing to live like other ordinary citizens.

Mzee Jomo Kenyatta, as he was referred to by then as a sign of endearment, was released in August 1961, whereupon, in early 1962, he led Kenya's delegation to the London Conference to negotiate the terms for Kenya's independence. In May 1963, KANU was victorious in the pre-independence elections, forming a preliminary government with Kenyatta as Prime Minister. Britain granted Kenya its Uhuru (independence) on December 12, 1963. The following year, Kenya's opposition voluntarily liquidated itself, effectively turning the country into a one-party state. A new republican constitution gave increasing authority to the president, including the dreaded power to arrest and detain his opponents, if he considered them a national risk. Both Oginga Odinga, Kenya's first vice president, and Tom Mboya would fall victim to this draconian law, as they parted company with Kenyatta over policies. This power got used and abused increasingly in equal measure, but perhaps more so under the rule of Daniel Arap Moi, who replaced Mzee Kenyatta upon his death in 1978.

Despite his 8-year incarceration, Kenyatta, like Nelson Mandela would do decades later, emerged from detention, not as a bitter revolutionary bent on revenge, but rather a pragmatist who confounded both his friends and antagonists by advocating a policy of tolerance and accommodation among different races and ethnicities. He rejected calls for nationalization of private properties, instead preached the "Harambee spirit" of togetherness. He also embraced private enterprise as the driving force, welcoming foreign direct investment (FDI), which acted as a catalyst for driving Kenya's economy to become the largest in Eastern Africa. But the growing economy didn't benefit everyone equally. Persistent complaints have continued over the distribution of land and other resources among the nation's different ethnic groups. Particular attention has been paid to the benefits received by groups that have produced a president such as the Kikuyu and Kalenjin, versus those that have not produced one such as the Luo, Luhya and Kamba. Many have questioned the legitimacy and methodology under which the Kenyatta and Moi families obtained excessive landholdings in a country teeming with thousands, if not millions of landless citizens.

Despite the acrimony over ethnic rivalry, Kenya followed the constitution to the letter and installed Vice-President Daniel Arap Moi as president upon the death of Mzee Jomo Kenyatta in 1978. He had joined KANU, the ruling party in 1964, and first served as Home Affairs Minister before being appointed Vice-President in 1967, replacing Oginga Odinga, a Luo who had fallen out with Mzee Kenyatta. Hailing from the small Kalenjin ethnic group of western Kenya, he was viewed as a non-threatening compromise over more hawkish candidates from the larger tribes. From the get-set, President Moi vowed to continue the policies of his fallen boss, akin to a hyena trailing in the footsteps of a lion on a hunt. This earned him the moniker of "Nyayo", the Swahili word for hyena. Once he settled in the job, however, Moi quickly consolidated his power by appointing fellow Kalenjin, then showed his mettle crushing opposition from the "big men" from larger tribes with a sense of entitlement. He also courted the army, in a relationship that aborted a coup attempt against his government in 1982.

His pro-western and free market policies paid-off handsomely in the so-called Africa's lost decade of the 1980's, turning Kenya's economy into a dynamo while others on the continent were floundering. But the 1990's ushered in a different kind of politics, as multitudes on the continent and elsewhere agitated towards economic reforms and multiparty elections after the end of the Cold War. President Moi held on to his position by cracking the whip on the opposition, jailing prominent leaders like Raila Odinga (son of Oginga Odinga), and renowned Kenyan Author Ngugi wa Thiongo. He won the first multiparty election in 1992 based on a simple majority that scored less than 50% in a crowded field, benefitting from a feuding opposition. Meanwhile, Kenya's economy began to faulter as institutions such as the World Bank and IMF abandoned him when he failed to carry out the prescribed reforms.

With serious internal opposition mounting, and the emergence of shadowy groups like Mwakenya threatening the security, Moi overplayed his hand, alienating his government from the ordinary mwanainchi, He prevailed in the 1997 elections, mired by violence in which many ethnic Kikuyu died. He managed to soldier on to the end of his 2nd and last term as allowed by the multiparty constitution through manipulation and adapting a carrot and stick approach to his detractors. By then, Moi's 24-year rule and KANU's uninterrupted stranglehold on the country had been tarnished by a government characterized by state-sponsored violence, and corruption, epitomized by the Goldenberg Scandal. As the 2002 elections approached, he nominated Uhuru Kenyatta, son of Mzee Jomo Kenyatta, to take KANU's mantle into the general election. However, Kenyatta was viewed as a lightweight, who would be heavily influenced by the Moi cabal. The party split into two factions, one of which joined the National Rainbow Coalition NARC).

This latter group (NARC) fielded Emilio Mwai Kibaki for president, a Kikuyu technocrat with degrees from Makerere University and the London School of Economics, who once served as Jomo Kenyatta's Finance Minister, and Moi's vice-president till they parted company. He won the election and was installed as Kenya's 3rd President in December 2002. Kibaki delivered a rousing inaugural speech in a wheelchair, following an auto accident he had gotten involved in during the campaign. His promise to create as many as 500,000 jobs every year, and to eliminate government corruption, got him cheers from the crowd, while Moi's motorcade was pelted with stones on his way to hand-over power. But Kibaki's regime turned out to be long on rhetoric, and short on delivery. Too much time was wasted over negotiations with leaders of the heads of parties constituting the NARC coalition jostling for power within the administration, while the promised fight against corruption took a back seat. To run for a second term in December 2007, Kibaki put together another coalition involving KANU, which was called the Party of National Unity (PNU). This party was pitted against another coalition called the Orange Democratic Movement (ODM), headed by Raila Odinga, in an election that was the closest in Kenya's history.

When the Electoral Commission announced Mwai Kibaki as the winner, ODM's Odinga refused to concede, defeat. Riots immediately broke out along ethnic fault lines, opening old rivalries, especially between the Kikuyu and Luo, which some saw as a plot by the Kikuyu to permanently shut the door to the presidency from other groups. There were perpetrators as well as victims initiated from all sides, including at the highest levels. By the time the late UN Secretary General Kofi Annan stepped in to mediate in February 2008, more than 1,000 innocent lives had been lost, thousands displaced from their homes, and countless properties destroyed. On February 28, 2008, Kibaki and Odinga signed a power-sharing agreement that would allow Kibaki to remain president, while Odinga would occupy the newly created position of Prime Minister. Although suspicions between the two antagonists remained, the delicate balance held on until the next election, which would expose the old rift once again. A new constitution agreed upon by voters was promulgated and signed into law on August 27, 2010. The document devolved power to the 47 counties into which the country was divided, and also addressed, among other things, the causes of the 2007 riots.

Kibaki turned over power to Uhuru Kenyatta, who had defeated Raila Odinga in a very close election in April 2013. However, Kenyatta's path to State House was laden with thorns. Back in 2010, the Gambian-born top prosecutor at the International Criminal Court, Fatou Bensouda, had preferred criminal charges on Uhuru Kenyatta and his running-mate, William Ruto. The charge sheet included, inter-alia, naming the pair, along with Radio announcer Joshua Sang, and top civil servant Francis Muthaura as perpetrators of the post-election violence following the 2007 elections which caused over 1,000 deaths and destruction of property. The nation's presidency remained in paralysis for some time while Kenyatta and Deputy President Ruto struggled to clear their names before the ICC. Although all the charges attributed to the named persons on the sheet were eventually dropped due to insufficient evidence, the case left an indelible stain. Many incidents were cited, where potential witnesses were bribed, while others were intimidated to prevent them from appearing before ICC prosecutors. For Kenyatta's second term in 2017, this became a rematch between him and Raila Odinga, with the two families' rivalry in full display before the whole world. The August 8, 2017 election became so contentious with allegations of manipulation and fraud which included the abduction and subsequent murder of the head of data-processing at the nation's Independent Electoral and Boundaries Commission. The Supreme Court, headed by Chief Justice David Maraga, annulled the results which initially gave Uhuru a narrow lead, and ordered another election to be held. This was an unprecedented move, and a first on a continent where incumbents rarely lose an election they organize. Uhuru prevailed by default after Odinga withdrew from the new election, indicating that the conditions his party had put forward for the rematch were not met.

Kenya is East Africa's largest and most dynamic economy which acts as an anchor in the region. Reforms inspired by the 2010 constitution, including the devolution of power to the 47 counties, away from the central government in Nairobi, have taken resources and services closer to the people. Although the economy faltered along with the global recession of 2008, it regained its footing, with GDP registering 5.7% in 2018, and expected to rise slightly to 5,9% in 2019, according to the outlook assessment by the World Bank Group. Conditions favoring this positive performance include the relaxation of political uncertainty, growth in private sector credit, strong in-flows of remittances, and continued low oil prices. Prudent fiscal management may bring down the deficit-to-GDP ratio to around 4.3%. The country has accumulated high levels of both domestic and external debt in the past decade, which has allowed for major infrastructure projects such as the Standard Gauge Railway (SGR), and modern dual-carriage highways. These are essential ingredients which will reduce bottlenecks in transportation of goods and services, allowing for further economic expansion.

In December last year, the president articulated what he referred to as the "Big Four" development priority areas of his presidency. He listed them as, manufacturing, universal healthcare, affordable housing, and food security, and last, but not least, social development. Regarding the Millennium Development Goals (MDG) set by the UN, the country has achieved some of the targets, including reduced child mortality, near universal primary school enrolment and a narrowing of the gender gap in education. Decentralization that followed the 2010 constitution has allowed the general population to utilize the services (especially health facilities) better. According to the most recent estimate in 2018, the country enjoys the highest internet penetration in Africa at 89%, compared to a continental average of around 40%. The corresponding figure for mobile telephony usage in Kenya was estimated at 80%. The data shows that the country is at the center of a dynamic revolution, and well positioned to take advantage of technological changes. Innovations such as Safaricom's M-Pesa, which introduced the world to mobile accounts a few years back, was a glaring example that not all modern innovations originate from the west. Kenya's challenge forward is channeling this dynamism into jobs for the burgeoning youth population taking place right now.

Kenya bade farewell to President Emilio Mwai Kibaki, a stalwart of many administrations since the independence era, who died on April 21, 2022, at age 91. The same year, the country witnessed another democratic change of the guard from President Uhuru Kenyatta to his former deputy, William Samoei Arap Ruto, with the August 8, 2022, election. Former President Uhuru Kenyatta had parted company with his deputy in favor of his 2017 opponent, Raila Odinga, in what came to be known as "the handshake". However, Mr. Ruto, who goes by the moniker, "the hustler", fought back against what he called dynastic forces bent on ring-fencing the top position in the country from smaller tribes. The election results were delayed through a supreme court petition in which Mr. Odinga accused the Independent Electoral and Boundaries Commission of declaring a fraudulent election in favor of Mr. Ruto, but in the end, the supreme court affirmed him as the winner. He became the nation's 5th president since independence in 1963.

CHAPTER 18

Tanzania left its mark on the world with studies about the origins of mankind in the Oluduvai Valley, conducted by Dr. Louis Leakey and his wife Mary Nicol, beginning in the 1950's. In an independent, but equally significant event, they were later followed by primatologist Dr. Jane Goodall who set up camp in Gombe Forest near Lake Tanganyika, and whose studies on chimpanzee use of tools confirmed man's close relationship with primates. The country has been traversed by man and beast alike for millions of years since the pre-historic era. Humanity as we know it, may owe our existence to that little ancestor, whose footsteps were discovered by Mary Leakey's team in 1976, entombed in the volcanic ashes at Laetoli.

The east coast of Africa has been plowed by many wayward sailors, including pirates, slave-traders, and explorers. Arabs sailed their dhows into those waters for perhaps a thousand years, long before Vasco da Gama cruised through in 1498, on his passage to India. The Arabs introduced Islam to the coastal region, which became the first foreign religion to take root. But they also undertook some evil deeds, the worst of which was slave-trade, which snatched innocent men, women and children from their families and cultures, hauling them off to far and unfamiliar places, to be sold off, and waste their lives away in bondage. The dominance of the Arabs was tempered by the arrival of Portuguese. Shortly after Vasco da Gama, in 1503, a Portuguese ship under Commander Rui Lourenco Ravasco arrived at Unguja island, the largest of the islands in the Zanzibari archipelago. His men seized twenty dhows, and killed about thirty-five people, all this done to force the ruler (Mwinyi Mkuu), to allow Portuguese ships to use the island as a supply station for food and water on their way to the orient. Outgunned and overpowered, the ruler acquiesced, and was even forced to pay tributes to the Portuguese. Perhaps, emboldened by their success, they ventured further north, where, in 1505, they captured the port of Mombasa (in present-day Kenya), establishing Fort Jesus. They spread their conquest to the neighboring island of Pemba in 1506, and by 1560, they had established Zanzibar town on Unguja island. During this time, they introduced two important crops, cassava (yuca), and cashew nuts, which they imported from Brazil. Later, cloves and other spices would be introduced, making Zanzibari planters wealthy.

Except for Mozambique to the south, the Portuguese had limited their rule to the coastal region and the islands. Their rule over Unguja lasted until 1652, when they were forcefully driven out by the Omanis. The last Portuguese were expelled from Pemba Island in 1695, while Fort Jesus returned to the Sultan of Oman in 1698. The Portuguese kept Mozambique on the south-east coast, and Angola on the south-west coast, from where they continued drawing their human cargo of slaves to ship to their new colony of Brazil to toil and perish in sugarcane plantations and mines. By the 18th Century, Arabs had penetrated the mainland, trading in slaves, ivory, and precious metals with African chiefs. But most of their slaves were transported to the Middle East and the Indian sub-continent. There, they were used in unsavory chores like leather tanning, salt mines, diving for pearls and even in the military of such countries as Oman. Others were utilized as agricultural help, while a few served as domestic servants for the well-to-do. European powers such as France joined the slave-trade on the east coast of Africa, shipping thousands of Africans to newly established colonies such as Mauritius, Seychelles, and Reunion, to work in sugarcane plantations.

Tanganyika, or German East Africa, as it was initially called, was created out of the same "Gunboat Diplomacy" of 1885 in which British East Africa (Kenya) was formed, after Chancellor Bismarck of Germany granted Karl Peters a charter for an East African Protectorate. Karl Peters was a young German maverick, smitten with imperial hubris for a German African empire. The year was 1884, and Chancellor Bismarck was hosting the Berlin Conference on the future of Africa, to demarcate the giant unexplored continent into spheres of influence. Karl Peters had arrived at Sultan Barghash's palace in Zanzibar, in 1884. Following in the footsteps of other European explorers of the day like Morton Stanley, he took the Bagamoyo route commonly used by Arab slave raiders, conversing the Sultan's mainland territories, as he and his two colleagues carried with them some blank forms and flags. Upon encountering an illiterate chief, they filled in his name and went about convincing him to accept protection from Germany by putting a mark or thumbprint on the form, and then gave him a German flag to hoist. Those who didn't accept these terms were threatened with grave consequences.

Seeing potential for Germany gaining territory in this manner but deterred by lack of food and other supplies which slowed his progress, Karl Peters decided to return to Berlin to sell the idea of an East African Protectorate to Chancellor Bismarck. The Chancellor bought into the proposition but wanted to know how it could be implemented. By this time, Sultan Barghash had heard the news about the annexation of his mainland territories and sent a protest message to the German Chancellor. When the Chancellor asked Karl Peters on how he (Bismarck) should respond to the Sultan, Peters suggested that the Chancellor should send a flotilla of German gunboats to a deep-water lagoon opposite the Sultan's palace in Zanzibar, ready to use force, if necessary. The gunboats arrived in August of 1885, with Bismarck's order that the Sultan cede his mainland territories to Germany, or face consequences. Meantime, news spread quickly by telegram to London, raising possibilities of a clash with Germany. To avert this prospect, British Prime Minister Lord Salisbury initiated a compromise that came to be known as the Heligoland Treaty. In the treaty, the tiny island of Heligoland was ceded to Germany in exchange for restricting their territorial interests in East Africa to an agreed-upon demarcation line stretching from the Indian Ocean coast, northwest towards Mt. Kilimanjaro, onwards to Lake Victoria, and then stretching westwards along parallel 1 degree south. Those lines have since marked the boundaries between present-day Tanzania, Kenya, and Ugandan boundaries. Karl Peters who had been granted a charter in February 1885, to run the East African Company, even leased the 10-mile coastal strip that had been left to the Sultan so that he could access the sea. A few uprisings by coastal Arabs were squashed by a combination of German soldiers and the British Navy. However, as in Lugard's case with the Imperial British East African Company, when Karl Peters' ability to run the territory on behalf of Germany faltered, the German government took it over, appointing him Imperial Commissioner.

Now the Germans had this vast territory to run, and like the British, they faced daunting problems on the ground. To ease transportation problems, in 1905, they launched construction of a central railway (mittellandbahn or Tanganjikabahn) from Dar-es-Salaam through Dodoma, and on to Tabora, and later extended to Kigoma on Lake Tanganyika. At the same time, they introduced cash crops like cotton, sisal and cashew nuts along the railway line, and coffee around the slopes of Mt. Kilimanjaro. The railway reached its terminus of 1,252 kilometers at Kigoma in 1914, shortly before the beginning of the First World War. German rule in Tanganyika was not a kind and gentle operation. The introduction of alien crops accompanied by forced labor on the plantations, galvanized the African people into resistance, which the Germans crushed with ruthless brutality.

In August 1905, an uprising known as the Maji-maji Rebellion, was started on the false rumor that a concoction of millet seeds and castor oil could neutralize German bullets by turning them into water (maji). More rumors followed, suggesting that people all over the country were uprooting cotton plants rather than tending them. This was followed by marauding crowds, who took the magic concoction, tied headbands of the millet plant, which symbolized the indigenous crop, then went on a rampage attacking German homes, killing a few of them in the process. The Germans acted very swiftly to crush and end the rebellion. By October, reinforcements of troops were sent in, but the German Commander, Gen. von Gotzen went even further. He hatched up a scorched-earth policy that would cause hunger and destruction to entire communities, in order to bring them into total submission. He instructed his troops to ransack the villages, thrush and burn food crops, even torch entire villages. Close to 250,000 Africans are estimated to have died from a combination of famine and diseases because of this.

The Maji Maji rebellion echoed the Herero uprising in Southwest Africa (Namibia) in 1904, during which Emperor William II assigned the task of quelling the uprising in the newly acquired German territory to Gen. Lothar von Trotha, with a reputation for brutality. Following a rinderpest epidemic that nearly wiped out their herds in 1896, the Herero made a last-ditch effort to sell the remnants of the cattle and pastureland to the German settlers so that they wouldn't lose everything. The rinderpest is eventually contained, and the cattle herds begin to thrive again, except they belong to German settlers, while the Herero hardly have any left. They realize they committed a great blunder. Now the Germans are even driving them out of their ancestral land. The only way to survive is to resist by driving out the intruders. Herero warriors went on a rampage, during which they attacked and killed some German settlers, with a view of scaring them enough to leave. They targeted only those capable of carrying arms, sparing women, children, and Europeans of other nationalities. The casualties didn't exceed 100.

When the news reached Berlin, a shocked Emperor William II chose to retaliate by selecting Gen. Lothar von Trotha, a man not known for handling his enemies with kid gloves, to go quell the uprising, and teach the natives a lesson they would never forget.

Von Trotha's troops pushed the Herero to the Waterberg plateau adjacent to the Kalahari Desert, and surrounded them on all sides, leaving them only one exit to the desert. With exception of coastal areas, most of Namibia is a semi-arid wasteland, forming the western edge of the 300,000 square mile Kalahari Desert. Von Trotha placed German guards near the entrance to the plateau, to stop the Herero from returning. In the ensuing scorching conditions, nearly 8,000 of the tribespeople perished. He followed this with an order to shoot any Herero found living within the German-occupied territory, the first known organized version of ethnic cleansing in the 20th century. Most of the world was shocked, which forced Germany to recall von Trotha from his command. But for all his transgressions, Emperor William II decorated him with high honors for his distinguished service to Deutschland. A 1911 census conducted in Namibia found that the population of Herero had reduced from 80,000 to 15,000 over the previous decade. The population of the Nama, another tribal group that resisted German rule, had reduced from 20,000 to 9,800 in the same period. Even Karl Peters himself was convicted in a Potsdam Court. His crime? He once flogged his African concubine, and then proceeded to hang her, together with his African assistant who had cheated on him with his lover.

After the 1st WW, Germany lost all its African territories which were transferred to Britain by the League of Nations. Britain retained Tanganyika but handed over the administration of Namibia to South Africa. Over the years, however, the country's indigenous population fared no better, as the Afrikaans regime in South Africa applied the same rigid racial rules of apartheid. Their economic lot failed to improve despite the discovery of diamonds in the country. In the early 1960's, a movement that began as the Ovambo Peoples' Organization casts a wider net to include other ethnic groups, morphing into the Southwest African Peoples Organization (SWAPO), led by Sam Nujoma. In coordination with the African National Congress (ANC) guerilla movement of South Africa led by Nelson Mandela, the two relentlessly battled the apartheid regime in Pretoria. A 1988 agreement that saw the withdrawal of Cuban soldiers from Angola, and South African troops from Namibia, finally paved the way for the independence of Namibia with SWAPO swept in power after Nujoma won the election with a 57% mandate. Sam Nujoma who turned 93 in 2022, served three terms until 2005, and remains an iconic figure for the Namibia people. He was replaced by

Hifikepunye Lucas Pohamba who served his two democratically allowed two terms, ending on March 21, 2015. Namibia's current president is Mr. Hage Geingob who assumed power on March 21, 2015, after a democratic election. President Pohamba stands out for being a member of that rare group of African leaders who have been awarded the Mo Ibrahim Prize of Achievement in African Leadership. The $5 million prize is only given to leaders who ascended to their positions in a credible democratic election, served their prescribed terms, and left power peacefully. Established in 2007 by Sudanese billionaire entrepreneur and founder of Celtel Communications, Mohamed Ibrahim, the prize has so far been awarded to only six African former presidents. They are Nelson Mandela of South Africa, Joachim Chissano of Mozambique, Festus Mogae of Botswana, Pedro Pires of Cape Verde, Hifikepunye Pohamba of Namibia, and the first female president on the continent, Ellen Sirleaf Johnson of Liberia. There's a bonus prize for guessing why east and central African leaders continue to be absent from this list.

The administration of Tanganyika was passed on to Britain following the Treaty of Versailles which stripped Germany of its territorial possessions in Africa, following vanquish in the 1st WW. Their governing style was the familiar indirect rule, already being implemented in the neighboring British territories of Kenya and Uganda. Traditional chiefs were encouraged and propped up with perks to support colonial administrators. Where there were none before, the British created their own. And, as in other places where they ruled, local councils and courts were established. A legislative council was formed, but Africans were not allowed to serve on it until the UN under whose mandate Britain had placed Tanganyika, enforced it after 1947. Then local leadership began to emerge in the early 1950's.

Julius Kambarage Nyerere was born on April 13, 1922, the son of a Zanaki tribal chief in Butiama, near the town of Musoma on the south-eastern shore of Lake Victoria. He started his primary education in Musoma at age 12, and later attended government secondary school in Tabora. He proceeded to Makerere University College in Uganda in the late 1940's and returned to Tanganyika to become a teacher, earning him the endearing title of "Mwalimu". After three years, he obtained a scholarship to the University of Edinburgh in Scotland, where he studied history and political economy for a masters' degree, becoming the first Tanzanian to obtain a degree from a British university. While there, he used his verbal and linguistic skills to translate a few Shakespeare plays into the Swahili language. Upon his return to Tanganyika, he reconstituted the old Tanganyika African Association into the Tanganyika African National Union (TANU) on July 7, 1954, turning the party into a mass movement. He was elected as president of the party. Provoked by the colonial administration to make a choice between teaching and political activities, he retorted that he was a teacher by choice, and a politician by accident.

Mwalimu Nyerere entered the Legislative Council in 1958 becoming its chief minister in 1960. The drumbeats for independence were sounding everywhere on the continent. By early 1961, the British granted the country internal self-government with Nyerere as Prime Minister. Tanganyika gained its full independence on December 9, 1961. Nyerere was elected president of the Republic of Tanganyika in 1962, Two years later, a Ugandan revolutionary named John Gideon Okello, led a revolution in Zanzibar, which overthrew the reign of Sultan Jamshid bin Abdullah, paving the way for the union between mainland Tanganyika and Zanzibar, creating the United Republic of Tanzania in 1964. Zanzibar had been granted its own independence by Britain in 1963. However, a manipulation of parliamentary procedures by minority Arab groups had resulted in their retention of power on the island, which they had inherited as an overseas territory of Oman. The Afro-Shirazi Party (ASP) which had won a plurality vote of 54% in the July 1963 elections, remained under-represented in parliament. The ASP allied itself with another indigenous people party, the Umma Party, then on January 12, 1964, John Okello a revolutionary mercenary from Uganda, mobilized between 600-800 men on Unguja island, Zanzibar's main island. They first seized guns from the police before proceeding to Zanzibar Town, where they toppled the Sultan and his minority government. The Sultan and his cabinet managed to flee on the royal yacht Seyyid Khalifa. Okello, a former policeman, with no known military training, had arrived on Pemba Island in 1959, claiming he was a Field Marshall from Kenya's resistance group, the Mau Mau. The revolution was followed by some bloodletting visited on Arabs and Asians with numbers estimated from a few hundreds to thousands. By Okello's orders, Europeans and other nationalities on the island were spared. Sheikh Abeid Amani Karume of the ASP was installed as the new president, with Abdulrahman Muhammad Babu as his deputy. During the fighting, Okello had dispatched them to the mainland for their safety. The revolution ended more than 200 years of Arab rule dominancy over Zanzibar. The country was renamed The Peoples' Republic of Zanzibar and Pemba, and one of Karume's first actions was to banish the Sultan and ban the Zanzibar National Party (ZNP), and Zanzibar and Pemba Peoples' Party (ZPPP), both Arab-dominated parties.

Mwalimu Nyerere took advantage of the revolution in Zanzibar, to lure and convince the new leaders to join mainland Tanganyika into a union. The result was the marriage of convenience that begat the United Republic of Tanzania on April 22, 1964. Julius Nyerere became president of the country, while Abeid Karume became the new nation's vice-president. However, the articles of the union were never widely publicized, and any criticism about it could result in prosecution and even imprisonment for endangering state security. That's what happened to Zanzibar's second president, Sheikh Aboud Jumbe and his chief minister, Seif Sharif Hamad, who wanted to push for more autonomy for Zanzibar. The two were harangued and ostracized, and eventually expelled from the ruling party, Chama Cha Mapinduzi (CCM).

President Nyerere was one of the founding members of the Organization of African Unity (OAU), whose charter was signed on May 25, 1963, in Africa Hall, Addis Ababa, Ethiopia. He was joined in this effort by the continent's other eminent pan Africanists such as Kwame Nkrumah of Ghana, Namdi Azikiwe of Nigeria, Ahmed Sekou Toure of Guinea, Abdel Nassar of Egypt, Jomo Kenyatta of Kenya, Milton Obote of Uganda, and host, Emperor Haile Selassie of Ethiopia. Nyerere used his stature and integrity to unite countries and communities alike. He was instrumental in the creation of the East African Community, (EAC), which bound Tanzania, Kenya and Uganda into a body that shared resources on economic and social services. Known as the Treaty for East African Cooperation, the EAC was established in 1967, with its headquarters in the city of Arusha, Tanzania. Although the Community set the tone for economic cooperation, both regionally and internationally, from the get set, it was beset with problems that would slowly suck and drain its energy, like a leech draws blood. First and foremost, Nyerere's socialist policy of Ujamaa was at loggerheads with Kenya's capitalistic approach of free enterprise. Uganda's position was a bit cloudy, with Milton Obote's "Move to the Left" strategy seriously resisted at home. While these forces could have been overcome, especially given the friendship Nyerere and Obote enjoyed between them, the coup de grace to the EAC's lifespan was delivered by the arrival of Idi Amin on the scene after toppling Obote. Amin's ideological incoherence, and provocative governance style left Nyerere flabbergasted to a point where he referred to Amin as "a snake in the grass that must be smoked out".

By 1977, all gloves between Nyerere and Amin were off, and it was quite clear they didn't belong in the same camp. The EAC was dissolved in 1977, and the assets once held jointly, were distributed among the three partner states. To-date, the only asset that still survives from that era is the East African Development Bank, with its headquarters in Kampala, Uganda. In December 1978, Amin provoked Nyerere's wrath by claiming a salient of Tanzanian territory around the Kagera river border. Nyerere seized this opportunity to send in battalions and tanks of Tanzania Peoples' Defense Forces, who collaborated with Ugandan exiles in flushing the scourge of Amin from Uganda. Nyerere welcomed many liberation movements which made Dar-es-Salaam home. The most prominent among them were, Nelson Mandela's ANC, Samora Machel's FRELIMO, and Robert Mugabe's ZANU.

Mwalimu Nyerere forged Tanzania into a strong and proud nation. Where most countries on the continent are still struggling with balancing gravitational forces of ethnicities that keep pulling them down, a Tanzanian will proudly wear that label instead of that of his tribe. Through his policy of Ujamaa, he emphasized humanness and respect for the total human being as opposed to material consumption.

But, while cooperative living created good neighbors, the forced moves of whole communities killed the entrepreneurial spirit that drives societies to succeed. By the time Nyerere voluntarily stepped down from the presidency in 1985, the Tanzanian economy was teetering near collapse stage. The country was saddled with a lot of external debt, incurred on the faith donors placed on the leader's integrity, not much else. Although the nation was united, it's Moses had retired, and it needed a Joshua to deliver them to the land of milk and honey.

After retirement from the presidency, Nyerere retained the chairmanship of Chama Cha Mapinduzi (CCM), the ruling party, effectively making him the kingmaker until 1990 when he relinquished power entirely. The president who never abused his position to accumulate wealth like most of his regional contemporaries and successors, retired to a small farm near his birthplace of Butiama. But, even in those quiet moments he cherished in his sunset years, he never shied away from service when duty called. He continued to be consulted by the high and mighty until his death in a London hospital on October 14, 1999. A devout catholic throughout his entire life, there is some internal mobilization among the catholic faithful in the region urging Rome to canonize him as a saint.

Tanzania's second post-independence leader was Ali Hassan Mwinyi, who was president for two terms beginning on November 5, 1985, to November 23, 1995. His tenure was characterized by an attempt to shift the country's orientation away from the failed socialist policies engineered by Julius Nyerere. It was also during Mwinyi's second term, that the country bowed to pressure from external donors, especially the World Bank and IMF, to open political space and allow other parties to compete against CCM. Referred to as Mzee Rukhsa (everything goes), he pushed for liberalization not only in the economy, but also in the nation's morals, provided people didn't break the law.

The nation's 3rd president was Benjamin William Mkapa, a professional journalist, trained at Makerere University in Uganda, and Columbia University, USA. He served two terms from November 23, 1995, to December 21, 2005. President Mkapa stands out as perhaps having had the most experience to qualify him for the position. Among his previous portfolios were press secretary to President Nyerere, High Commissioner to Nigeria, High Commissioner to Canada, Ambassador to the US, and Minister of Foreign Affairs. President Mkapa pushed for further liberalization and divestiture of the economy, including the sale of the National Bank of Commerce, the largest bank in the country, controlled by the government. He also called for transparency, which he demonstrated by declaring his assets and those of his family.

Jakaya Mrisho Kikwete became Tanzania's 4th president on December 14, 2005. Prior to assuming the highest position in the land, he served as Foreign Minister for his predecessor, Mr. Mkapa during his entire tenure in office. As president, Mr. Kikwete was heavily involved in bringing peace to the hot spots in the region, especially DRC and Burundi, and the revival of the new and expanded East African Community. On the downside, there were many high-profile cases of malfeasance during Mr. Kikwete's term of office, including the Governor of the Central Bank, and a former Prime Minister. His pet project, the Southern Agricultural Corridor of Tanzania (SAGCOT) which sought to support smallholder farmers while promoting venture capital into the sector, was later watered down by his successor, who favored more government participation.

The 5th president of Tanzania was John Pombe Magufuli, who assumed power on November 5, 2015. Referred to as "the bulldozer" for his abrasive leadership style, Mr. Magufuli instituted drastic measures aimed at forcing government agencies to live within their means. The doctrinaire ex-seminarian not consumed with worldly excesses, championed austerity by reducing his own salary from $15,000 to $4,000 a month. He also curtailed wasteful government travel, reduced the size of missions such as representation at the UN in New York, and forced agencies to purchase cheaper vehicles. In 2015, he suspended the country's independence celebrations in favor of engaging the population to clean up their localities. Magufuli suspended the registration of foreign merchant ships, alleging that ships carrying the country's flag were being used for carrying drugs and other contraband merchandise. The man with a short- hotwired fuse and a flare for dramatics, known for firing people on the spot, instilled fear that put most heads of government agencies on tenterhooks, unsure where the ax may fall next. President Magufuli is credited with having pushed for increased use of the Kiswahili language in the SADC countries, and in the EAC countries, where the language is already widely spoken. Despite holding a Ph D in chemistry, the doctrinaire president stubbornly refused to believe the seriousness of the Covid-19 pandemic, which he dismissed as nothing more than a new strain of the common cold. His stubbornness kept Tanzania out of the campaign to receive globally approved vaccines, which caused many citizens to die unnecessarily. In the end, when he contracted Covid himself, his unvaccinated condition could not offer any resistance to the deadly virus. He was rushed to Nairobi, Kenya, where doctors could not rescue him. He was rushed back to Dar-es-Salaam, Tanzania, where he succumbed to the virus on March 17, 2021, a fact that was never officially admitted.

In line with the country's constitution, the vice-president, Ms. Samia Suluhu Hassan, a Zanzibari native, was sworn in as the nation's 6th president on March 19, 2021. She is a member of the Chama Cha Mapinduzi party (CCM), which has ruled Tanzania since its independence in 1961. She joined a small and rare group of female heads of state on the continent, that includes Sirleaf Johnson of Liberia, and Joyce Banda of Malawi, although other women have occupied these positions in temporary acting capacities.

Tanzania enjoyed a high economic growth in the range of 6-7% over the past decade, according to the 2019 World Bank Economic Outlook. This performance reduced the poverty rate, but the impact was negated by a high birth rate that kept the absolute number of the poor on the rise. President Magufuli's no-nonsense style of intolerance towards corruption, reassured the public that malfeasance can at least be managed. Although 2018 GDP figures were held back due to rebasing, the most recent data shows that the economy was softening somewhat, compared to the prior years. FDI had declined, partly driven by the president's insistence that mining companies must process more ore domestically instead of exporting raw minerals. The current account deficit increased from 2.9% of GDP to 4.4% during the year ending December 2018. Headline Inflation held stable at around 3%, and the country's reserves were considered adequate, at $5 billion, equivalent to 4.9 months of imports.

The country has made many positive strides towards domestic self-sufficiency in energy production in the recent past. Tanzania made headline news in 2010 when the discovery of a major deposit of natural gas in the Lindi region was announced. It has now been confirmed that the nation has 57 trillion cubic feet of proven natural gas reserves, 49.5 trillion of which are offshore in the Indian Ocean. Since the discovery, many plans have been put into action towards the exploitation of this major energy resource. The Tanzanian Petroleum Development Corporation has collaborated with the BG Group (a subsidiary of Royal Dutch Shell), together with Equinor, ExxonMobil, and Ophir Energy, to build a giant LNG onshore export terminal in Lindi, located about 100 kilometers south-east of Mtwara Town. On October 10, 2022, the Tanzanian president, Samia Suluhu Hassan, and her Kenyan counterpart, William Ruto, agreed to fast-track the construction of a 600-kilometer natural gas pipeline that will transport gas from Dar-es-Salaam to Mombasa on the Kenyan coast. Tanzania is also jointly involved with Uganda, in the construction of the East African Crude Oil Pipeline (EACOP), which will transport Uganda's oil from Hoima in western Uganda, to the Tanzanian Indian Ocean port of Tanga.

In a related development, in April 2018, the government commissioned a US344 million gas-powered 168-megawatt plant outside the capital of Dar-es-Salaam. This, together with the 2,100-megawatt hydro-electric plant that opened in July the same year at Stiegler's Gorge in Selous Game Reserve, were game-changers in the nation's path towards energy self-sufficiency. Until then, the nation of 55 million was getting by on a mere 1,400 megawatts of mainly hydro-powered electricity, whose supply was sometimes interrupted by severe droughts.

CHAPTER 19

Although the era of the "big man" has been fading in most countries on the African continent, it remained a mainstay in a few, such as Zimbabwe, where the late Robert Mugabe turned a once blossoming food basket into a wasteland. Nevertheless, the boy-wonder of the African liberation movement remained an enigma until his death on September 6, 2019, in a Singapore hospital. He was both celebrated by his admirers, while at the same time vilified by his detractors in equal measure for tarnishing the good name of African liberation by smearing and hijacking it with self-aggrandizing actions. As Muammar Qaddafi did in Libya until he met his inglorious death hiding in a sewer pipe in 2011, Robert Mugabe (or Uncle Bob, as he was popularly known on the continent) dominated Zimbabwe like the sun rules the sky.

In November 2017, Uncle Bob was forced to leave the presidency in a humiliating manner when senior military generals of the Zimbabwe Army, appalled by the paralysis arising from rivalry over Mugabe's succession, decided to intervene for the sake of the country's stability. The triangular rivalry started with Mr. Mugabe's second wife, South African-born Grace Ntombizodwa Marufu, whom he married in 1996.

She was his secretary, and at age 31, was 41 years his junior. Mr. Mugabe's first wife, Ghanaian-born Sally Hayfron had died on January 27, 1992. Grace, who had earned herself the unflattering nickname of Gucci Grace, on account of her penchant for indulging in expensive items while her compatriots swam in squalor, got increasingly ambitious as her husband's age advanced. Not satisfied with her role as First Lady, she plunged into politics, serving as the head of the women's wing of ZANU/PF, and made headlines when she received an unearned PhD, conferred upon her by none other than her husband, the Honorary Chancellor of the University of Zimbabwe. Her new visibility enabled her to target longtime Vice President, Joyce Mujuru, whose husband, Gen. Mujuru was killed in a suspicious fire at his farm. Grace launched a vicious campaign against the VP, dragging her name in the mud, and insinuating that she was working behind the scenes to oust the country's beloved president. Once Mrs. Mujuru was removed and expelled from the party, Grace turned her guns on Mnangagwa who had replaced Joyce Mujuru as VP. It appears, in Mnangagwa, she had met her match in tenacity. When Mr. Mugabe caved in and accepted her demands to fire the new VP, it became clear whom Grace wanted to fill that spot. After he was fired, Mnangagwa made a tactical withdrawal from the country, using his absence to coordinate with fellow generals in the country to plan the ouster that ended President Mugabe's 37-year reign. From then on, the once self-assured nonagenarian president of independent Zimbabwe, became crest-fallen and dejected, not unlike Cecil, the one-time domineering and oldest lion in the country, shot and killed by American Dentist, Walter Palmer, on July 2, 2015, in Hwange National Park. Following the ouster, his daily activities were reduced to enjoying a bowl of his favorite millet porridge for breakfast in the sprawling Blue Roof mansion, located in the leafy Borrowdale suburb of Harare. Close to his end, Uncle Bob was confined to a hospital in faraway Singapore, where he had become a frequent visitor in recent years.

At 95, he was engaged in a desperate attempt to defy natural gravity and save his life from a rumored terminal cancer, thought to have been prostate. Despite a near empty treasury, no expense was spared when it came to treating Uncle Bob, all that happening in a country where most of his compatriots could neither afford an aspirin for a headache, nor a decent meal of their staple sadza. The manner of his exit, pushed aside by the very army officers who once adored him and looked upon him with the reverence of a fatherly figure, left him bitter to the very end. In the July 2018 election that confirmed his successor Emmerson Mnangagwa in power, the first in which he was not on the ballot since taking power, he vowed to vote for the opposition which he had spent years brutalizing, instead of his ZANU/PF which had abandoned him. He went to the extent of giving instructions snubbing burial in the sacred Heroes Acres Burial ground in Harare after his death. He was finally laid to rest in his ancestral village of Kutama on September 28, 2019, after consultation with his widow, Grace, and his relatives. Now President Mnangagwa has a dilemma on his hands. Does he finish the mausoleum originally meant for Mugabe's glorification and reserve it for himself, or redeem his soul by assigning it to one of the "unknown" vagabonds who starve and die on Harare's streets every day because of ZANU/PF misrule?

By the time Robert Mugabe took the reins of power as Prime Minister of an independent Zimbabwe in Rufaro Stadium on April 18, 1980, the country had endured nearly 100 years of colonialism and white domination, making it the longest British rule in Africa. First toasted as a liberator with a reconciliatory agenda, once in power, his domineering and uncompromising style soon placed him on a collision course with his erstwhile enthusiastic supporters, rendering the former freedom fighter a pariah in many capitals, especially those of western democracies.

Robert Gabriel Mugabe was born on February 21, 1924, at Kutama Roman Catholic Mission, in Zvimba District of then Southern Rhodesia. When Mugabe was a young boy, his father Gabriel Matibiri, a carpenter went to work at a Jesuit mission in South Africa, and never returned home. His mother Bona, a teacher, was left to cater for Mugabe and his three siblings. He attended Kutama College under the tutorage of Jesuit Father O'Hea, the Director of the school. Father O'Hea became an early influence on the young boy, whose intellect the teachers recognized early on. From Father O'Hea, he learned that all people should be treated equally, and educated to the best of their abilities. Then for nine years, he practiced what he had learned by teaching in local mission schools before proceeding to Fort Hare University in South Africa, then a bastion of future African nationalist liberators, including Nelson Mandela.

After graduation with a bachelors' degree in History and English in 1951, he returned to Southern Rhodesia and taught in secondary schools near his home. By 1953, he had earned a bachelors' degree in education by correspondence, and moved to Northern Rhodesia (Zambia), where he taught at Chalimbana Training College. From here, he moved to Ghana, and taught at St Mary's Teacher Training College, where he met his first wife Sarah Hayfron (Sally), whom he would marry in 1961. Inspired by Kwame Nkrumah's successes in steering Ghana towards independence in 1957, Mugabe returned to Southern Rhodesia in 1960, but the Rhodesia he had left behind was changing fast with an explosion of white settlers, encouraged by a minority government which was pushing Africans from their ancestral lands. Angered by all this mistreatment, Mugabe embraced Marxism, and became immersed in liberation movements, determined to secure independence led by leaders from the majority people of his country. He was first elected Publicity Secretary of the National Democratic Party. His party took a more militant approach after Joshua Nkomo's Zimbabwe African People's Union (ZAPU), appeared too ineffective to address the Africans' immediate demands on the government. However, his brazen rhetoric and anti-government statements placed him in direct confrontation with the white minority government headed by Ian Smith. Mugabe, in collaboration with other militants from Joshua Nkomo's ZAPU, formed their own resistance movement called the Zimbabwe African National Union (ZANU) in 1963.

Then, in 1964, he was arrested, tried, and convicted on charges of sedition, and sent to prison, first to Hwahwa, then to Sikombela Detention Center, and finally to Salisbury Prison, in all for a total stay of ten years. While in prison, Ian Smith attempted a unilateral declaration of independence (UDI), in 1965, which Britain refused to recognize.

Mugabe used his time in jail to polish up on his academic skills by acquiring higher degrees from various institutions. His eloquence earned him the moniker of "thinking man's guerilla". In 1966, Ian Smith refused to grant him permission to go and attend the burial of his young son who had died of malaria in Ghana. Close observers of Mugabe attribute his animosity towards the white community in Zimbabwe to this incident. Mugabe escaped from Smith's grip in 1974, after being allowed to go to attend a conference in Lusaka, Zambia. He crossed into neighboring Mozambique, where Samora Machel was, already fighting a protracted guerilla war against Portuguese rule under the umbrella of the Front for Liberation of Mozambique (FRELIMO). Mr. Mugabe organized A guerilla army within ZANU, whose members started launching incursions into Southern Rhodesia against the minority regime, targeting government military and economic institutions that would cripple the regime's operational capacity. By 1979, with Rhodesia's economy battered, and international pressure brought to bear on British Prime Minister Margaret Thatcher, both Ian Smith and Robert Mugabe were invited to Lancaster House to negotiate the terms for transferring power to majority rule.

One of the thorniest issues of the negotiations was the transfer of land occupied by settlers under forced evictions, back to its African owners. The Conservative Government in London had agreed to finance a program under the terms of "willing buyer/willing seller". However, most farmers, already reaping rewards from cheap African labor, were not ready to give up their comfortable lifestyles to suit the whims of revolutionaries. Moreover, those who were ready to participate, did so by inflating the values of their farms so much, so that the funds budgeted could never suffice. For almost a decade, the drip-drip program dragged on at snail speed, causing a lot of anxiety and frustration among the Zimbabwean majority who aspired to enjoy the fruits of their independence. But when the Labor Government took over in 1997, Prime Minister Tony Blair, scrapped this program, and Zimbabweans were left to their own devices. It was this cancellation that infuriated Mugabe and ZANU, prompting him to order the so-called "land grabs" from white farmers beginning in the early 2000's.

Mr. Mugabe's derision for the British Premier was so palpable, that at one Commonwealth Heads of Government Meeting, he lashed at him, saying,

"We do not need Britain, you can keep your Britain, and I'll keep my Zimbabwe".

Unfortunately, Mugabe turned out to be a David attempting to slay Goliath with a broken slingshot. Although Zimbabwe's economy had taken a beating from ZANU's protracted guerrilla war, Mugabe took over a country that had a relatively well-developed infrastructure and agricultural sector. Compared to most sub-Saharan countries of the "lost decade", Zimbabwe was the envy of the region. At his inauguration in April 1980, Mwalimu Julius Nyerere of Tanzania reminded him with these prophetic words,

"You have inherited a jewel, don't tarnish it".

But tarnish it, he did, and then some. Zimbabwe's first decade of independence was characterized by international goodwill at the beginning, ranging from Robert Mugabe having the famous Four O'clock Tea with the Queen of England, to a Rose Garden photo op with a beaming President Jimmy Carter at the White House. Foreign aid which had been suspended as part of the sanctions to force Ian Smith to surrender power, was restored. The agricultural sector and industrial production also benefitted as the white community who controlled most of the commercial sector, sensed a lull in the incendiary rhetoric used by the new president. With aid flowing in, Mugabe built schools and hospitals to improve standards for the black population. At the same time, he was pre-occupied with fending off competition from former freedom fighters like Joshua Nkomo. In 1982, following clashes between ex-combatants from the ZANU ruling party dominated by Shona, and Joshua Nkomo's ZAPU, of predominantly Ndebele, Mr. Mugabe ordered the army's Fifth Brigade, trained by North Koreans, to quell riots in Matabeleland in an operation dubbed "Gukurahundi", (the rain that washes out the chaff). This military expedition dragged on for nearly five years, resulting in the death of an estimated 20,000 of mostly Ndebele. Although the numbers pale in comparison to Rwanda's genocide, nevertheless, the gruesome nature of the operation had the tell-tell signs of ethnic cleansing and was condemned in many quarters both at home and abroad. Mr. Emmerson Mnangagwa, the current president of Zimbabwe was the security minister at the time. To avert similar future clashes, Joshua Nkomo's ZAPU agreed to join an un-holly alliance with ZANU, creating ZANU/PF, but the mistrust remained.

Land Reform in Zimbabwe was at the heart of the guerrilla war of the 1970's. However, when Tony Blair's Labor government reneged on the terms of the Lancaster Agreement in which, inter-alia, the British would fund the land purchases from white farmers, Mr. Mugabe vowed to fast track the program with or sans British help. His argument was that the government of Zimbabwe was not obligated to pay for land which the white settlers had confiscated from Africans.

Prior to the arrival of Europeans in the late 19th century, land ownership in Zimbabwe, as elsewhere in Africa, was mostly on a communal basis. Individual families were allocated specific parcels where they could grow crops and raise a few animals to sustain a simple agrarian life. If another family encroached, the village chief settled the dispute, preserving peace within the community.

Then along came the Europeans, beginning with Cecil Rhodes in 1885. He had made a huge fortune in the diamond mines of Kimberly in South Africa and wished to expand his empire by seeking more fortunes further north. He began his quest by dispatching his business partner, Charles Rudd to meet with Chief Lobengula of the Ndebele, dangling a few trinkets, while asking him to guarantee Rhodes a monopoly of mineral rights in his vast territory. Upon agreement, the chief would be paid a monthly stipend of 100 British pounds. In addition, he would be given 1,000 Martini Henry rifles and 100,000 rounds of ammunition, only half of the rifles and ammunition deliverable before the agreement. It didn't take long for Chief Lobengula to realize that he'd been taken for a ride. Soon after acceding to the terms, Rhodes formed a company, the British South African Company, applied for a charter from the British government, as the first wave of white settlers started moving in, acquiring big chunks of land by pushing out the natives. On September 26, 1890, Rhodes hoisted the Union Jack in a small town they named Salisbury, in honor of then British Prime

Minister, Lord Salisbury. Chief Lobengula and his warriors went from one disastrous defeat to another, as they desperately attempted to uproot and expel the new invaders, who outgunned them, thanks to the backing of the mighty British army.

The British South African Company run the Rhodesian colony on behalf of the British until 1923, after which it became self-governing, with rigid racial laws that were a mirror image of apartheid in next door South Africa. Therefore, when Robert Mugabe and Joshua Nkomo launched their freedom fighting armies under ZANU and ZAPU, respectively, their circumstances were no different from those faced by Nelson Mandela and his comrades in the African National Congress (ANC). In fact, they had common enemies who often coordinated their efforts to fight and frustrate any attempt to liberate any of the two white-ruled neighboring countries. Likewise, the leaders of ZANU/PF closely collaborated with those of the ANC, sharing vital intelligence on operations, and sheltering their respective operatives wherever and whenever it was necessary. It is no secret that Mugabe's fledgling regime was continually given a lifeline by Pretoria after the apartheid regime was scrambled, even when the rest of the world had long abandoned Mugabe. Zimbabwe, Zambia, Tanzania, and Mozambique were the frontline states which formed a bulwark against the apartheid regime in South Africa, willing to risk their territories against a potential invasion from the superior and better-equipped army of South Africa. Incursions were commonplace in Mozambique, Lesotho and Swaziland, often in pursuit of ANC militants of Umkhonto we Sizwe.

South Africa currently hosts more than 3 million economic refugees from Zimbabwe. Most were forced to flee Zimbabwe beginning in the early 2000's after Mugabe seized the large white farms where the vast majority were employed. But, despite the xenophobia that followed hordes of immigrants who flocked to South Africa following the end of apartheid, Zimbabweans do not appear to be in the crosshairs of the rioters targeting the "Makwerekwere" (foreigners). This strong and derogatory term is mainly reserved for immigrants from the rest of sub-Saharan Africa, especially Somalis, Nigerians and Congolese, who have brought their entrepreneurial skills to the underserved townships of major South African cities such as Johannesburg, Pretoria and Cape Town. Part of the tolerance for Mugabe and Zimbabweans in general, stems from the fact that they share common bloodlines. The Ndebele are an indigenous group extending beyond the Zimbabwe border into South Africa. Their language is one of the eleven official languages spoken and broadcast on South African Broadcasting Corporation, (SABC).

By the late 90's, the white community in Zimbabwe constituted less than 1% of the population but controlled more than 70% of the country's arable land. Mr. Mugabe's blunder in land redistribution laid as much with the confiscation, as it was with the recipients. Most of the new owners who inherited these large farms had neither the experience in farming, nor the interest. Many were Mugabe's former comrades-in-arms, appointed civil servants, who were happy to lavish themselves with palatial homes and expensive cars, and harvest the fruits of their guerrilla sweat in Harare. Upon acquiring the farms, assets such as tractors, ploughs and even irrigation systems were auctioned off, as they installed their inexperienced relatives to manage the farms on their behalf. Meanwhile, following the trend in the region, the population was being decimated by HIV. This was a result of migrant labor to the South African mines who contracted it in unsanitary dormitory environments where they shared infected needles and partners, then imported the ailments to their countries. Mugabe was also facing unrest from the trade union movement causing endless labor strikes that started hurting the economy. However, the coup de grace was delivered by the Bretton Woods institutions (IMF & World Bank) which pulled out of Zimbabwe soon after Mugabe authorized the seizure of white-owned farms. In the 2002 elections, Mugabe secured victory by engaging war veterans to beat up and harass the opposition and other members of the public showing a semblance of anti-Mugabe retention of power.

The absence of the multilateral institutions, coupled with sanctions from western countries put a chokehold on the economy, creating major shortages and escalation in the inflation rate. The education sector, once among the best in the region, deteriorated to a point where students in primary schools wrote in the dust for luck of exercise books, while those in secondary schools couldn't take exams due to lack of paper. The period between 1999 and 2009 saw food production drop by 45%, manufacturing fell by 29% in 2005 alone, followed by another drop of 26% in 2006. Unemployment rose to 80%. The inflation rate in Zimbabwe registered a record that had never been experienced anywhere else in the world, peaking at 79,600,000,000 % per month in November 2008. This unfathomable inflation was mainly caused, by, among other things, the Reserve Bank of Zimbabwe's continuous printing of currency during severe shortages of goods and services. As a check on hyperinflation, the government experimented with dollarization of the economy. This involved an injection of large sums of dollars into the economy, mostly from international transfers. The central bank had no effective control because the money was outside the banking system. The authorities gradually found out that, without control of their own monetary policy, coupled with a lack of property rights, and a conducive business environment, dollarization alone was no panacea. The experiment was terminated on February 25, 2019, as the country re-launched a new Zimbabwe dollar.

The country's political landscape was getting increasingly challenging for Mugabe with the growth of opposition parties. His survival rested on destabilizing them through intelligence and at times, raw violence. Morgan Tsvangirai, the leader of the largest opposition party, the Movement for Democratic Change (MDC), became Mugabe's main target. In 2005, Operation Murambatsivina, a disguised anti-opposition drive disrupted life for an estimated 700,000 people in cities by destroying temporary shelters and properties, forcing many to be homeless. City dwellers formed the bulk of Mugabe's opposition. In a further escalation, of violence and intimidation in anticipation of elections, on March 12, 2007, Morgan Tsvangarai was severely beaten by ZANU/PF zealots, leaving him bleeding and taking shelter in the Dutch Embassy in Harare. The operation was widely condemned both at home and abroad, although Mugabe appeared to relish in it, going so far as claiming that he had added another "degree of violence" to his already swelling list of academic papers.

The Zimbabwean economy was projected to contract by about 7.5%

during 2019, according to the World Bank Group. Poverty has become more widespread, both in cities and rural areas, the latter mainly affected by El Nino induced drought conditions. Sharp increases in food prices have hampered the ability of the urban poor to purchase enough food for an adequate diet. Poverty is estimated to have risen from 29% in 2018 to 34% in 2019. Maize (corn) production, which forms the base of the staple diet, was reduced to half its level for the previous year, while mineral production fell by 27%. Inflation was roaring again, reaching 319% by July 2019, a result of monetization of previous fiscal deficits and currency distortions. The fiscal deficit which stood at 4.9% of GDP, was expected to reduce slightly to 4.5% in 2020, while real GDP growth was projected to pick up and grow at around 2.7% per annum driven by the agricultural sector with the return of rain. However, the economy, and poverty in general, will remain vulnerable as inflationary forces will linger on. The international community has been lukewarm towards the Mnangagwa regime, whom some view as a masked face of his predecessor. The arrival of Covid-19 in December 2019 further dumped hopes of a quick recovery for a country like Zimbabwe, already in dire straits. Inflation remains in triple digits, estimated at around 213% during 2022. The World Bank lending program is currently in limbo, due to arrears. The Bank's role is limited to technical assistance and analytical programs through Trust Funds. External debt is estimated at 76% of GDP, of which 70% is in arrears. Trade integration has declined, while FDI remains low, hampering technology transfer, limiting modernization of the economy.

FINAL NOTE

This book is not meant to be a kiss and tell, but rather a walk through the meandering rough path colonial sub-Saharan Africa has taken to arrive where it is today. It's been a monumental journey that required resilience and dogged determination. Although the initial baby steps were taken, and the path well-choreographed, it was a slippery one, and some stumbled along the way. Pioneers like Kwame Nkrumah, Namdi Azikiwe, Felix Houphouet-Boigny, Haile Selassie, Julius Nyerere, Jomo Kenyatta and later, Nelson Mandela, all held the door open for us to walk through and shone the torch towards the promised land. They put on a good fight, but their mortal nature instinctively required another cohort of leaders to pick up the baton where they left off. The author excluded Emperor Haile Selassie reign, because Ethiopia was never colonized, (although Italy attempted from October 1935 to February 1937), while Nelson Mandela's was a struggle against an oppressor from within, which took place long after South African independence. Although time and space did not allow us to examine and lay out the case for every country in the region, suffice it to say that in the grand scheme of things, the stories would have had a common theme. From the gallant men of the independence decade (1957-1967), none is still alive. Among the last to exit the world stage since this book was started, we bade farewell to former President of Kenya, Mzee Daniel Arap Moi, whose death occurred on February 4, 2020, aged 96 years. Kenneth Kaunda of Zambia, the last of the Mohicans, passed away on June 21, 2021, in Lusaka, Zambia at age 97. Sam Nujoma who carried the torch for Namibia, among the cohort that received independence later, is still alive and well at 93 years young as of this writing on October 16, 2022. To all these pioneers, we say Thank You.

Africa is a huge place, second only to Asia in terms of land mass. To put it into context, at 11.5 million square miles, one can fit nearly three United States of Americas (3.8 million square miles) inside the African continent. With a size like that, and given its diversity in people and ethnicities, no single set of rules can deliver a solution to the potpourri of problems that exist. But that's true in many other places too. As recently as twenty years ago, Africa was ignored in almost every forum, its contribution marginalized, its people denigrated and shunned. Today, however, change is in the air, as countries such as China, Japan and South Korea, lead the way in courting Africans to be their partners, while the US and the EU, the traditional partners and colonizers scramble to showcase their wares and skills to gain or retain a foothold on the continent. There's renewed interest in the region from many stakeholders. While a few skeptics may call it neo-colonialism, the truth is that the Africans themselves have driven this initiative by their relentless quest to find new ways of tackling problems that have oftentimes appeared intractable. New trade deals and economic realignments have forced traditional partnerships to compromise or miss out altogether. Nothing can be taken for granted anymore. New modern highways and railways are springing up in places never touched by development before, while telephone technology and the internet have enabled communication to unite communities at a level not anticipated even ten years ago. All this, plus a change in attitudes from outsiders on how they view and treat Africans, have combined to boost the momentum necessary. Change comes slowly everywhere and is sometimes resisted by both instigators and recipients alike. But in the end, change is inevitable for any society to progress. Africans must be assertive in a competitive world. The continent cannot afford to remain the source of primary raw materials that others churn into pricey manufactured goods then turn around and dump them on the same continent. African leadership must refrain from "kupalappalanya", a Luganda word that describes someone adept at using unconvincing excuses to justify why his performance always falls short of expectations. The long-suffering citizens of that beautiful continent deserve better.

Slavery and colonialism may be gone from the continent, but their impact and ramifications such as the unfair distribution of land, and subjugation of one group by another, encouraged by, and rampant during colonialism, still linger on in so many countries. Extreme income inequality, and lack of job opportunities have pushed vulnerable young people, to seek employment abroad, based on empty promises. Once they leave the safety of their families, especially young girls, unscrupulous men, trade them like merchandise, turning them into sex workers, with the attending consequences of deadly diseases like HIV and debased dignity. It's clear that many leaders in the region have not made maximum effort towards resolving such issues. Human rights records as well as people's mandates continue to be violated and abused to cater for individual egos. Corrupt regimes deprive their people of the means to survive at home, pushing them to take risks over uncharted territories such as crossing the Mediterranean Sea on rickety vessels. A lack of respect at home also translates into lack of respect abroad.

All humanity shares a common destiny in this one world, Environmental damage, or a new disease in one little corner of the globe eventually affects everyone. Nothing could illustrate the common plight of humanity better than the current pandemic caused by the coronavirus. First detected in Wuhan City in Hubei Province of China in December 2019, the virus has now engulfed the entire world, leaving death and untold suffering in its wake to both the mighty and downtrodden. Thanks to the spectacular skills in modern science and technology, complimented by global cooperation, the pandemic's catastrophic devastation has now been reduced to manageable levels. The lessons from the Covid-19 pandemic can also be applied to injustice in society.

Injustice in one society translates to injustice everywhere. Humanity must contend with the fact that, even with the best of NASA and Space-X technologies, the bulk of mankind will continue to inhabit Mother Earth in the foreseeable future. It is, therefore, imperative to realize, that we're destined to rise or sink together.